# EVERYBODY'S MAN

# EVERYBODY'S MAN

*A BIOGRAPHY OF*

# JIMMY STEWART

## JHAN ROBBINS

 Robson Books

FIRST PUBLISHED IN GREAT BRITAIN IN 1985
BY ROBSON BOOKS LTD., BOLSOVER HOUSE,
5-6 CLIPSTONE STREET, LONDON W1P 7EB.
COPYRIGHT © 1985 BY JHAN ROBBINS

British Library Cataloguing in Publication Data
Robbins, Jhan
    Everybody's man: a biography of Jimmy Stewart. 1.
Stewart, James 1908- 2. Moving-picture actors and
actresses – United States – Biography. I. Title
791.43'028'0924    PN2287.S68

ISBN 0-86051-314-9

Printed in Hungary

TO PENNY, TOM, MEG, DAVID AND KATIE.
*Thank you for being my children.*

# CONTENTS

# FOREWORD

I have spoken with more than one hundred fifty men and women in Hollywood; Indiana, Pennsylvania; Washington, D.C.; and other places where Jimmy Stewart has lived and visited. The result is an oral history profile of a unique, much-loved actor who has set high standards for all of us.

I couldn't find anyone who didn't like Jimmy. Over and over, I kept hearing versions of a remark made originally by Ronald Reagan: "I often wished I were just like him." It didn't matter if the person were young, middle-aged or old. For more than fifty years, moviegoers have singled him out as being the most trusted and admired Hollywood superstar. His devoted fans have always pointed to his inspiring quality of decency. His movies, often rereleased and shown on television, still draw millions of viewers.

Harry Truman once said: "If Bess and I had a son, we'd want him to be just like Jimmy Stewart."

Carol Burnett: "What a swell brother he'd make. A folksy elder statesman. Another Will Rogers."

Gloria Stewart, his wife of thirty-five years: "Jimmy's the husband every woman wants—a dear, loving, earnest human being."

Nancy Reagan: "When I was growing up, I had a giant crush

on Jimmy. I pasted his picture on the cover of my school note-book. I wished he would show up and take me to the prom."

Natalie Wood played Stewart's daughter in *The Jackpot*. Shortly before her death, she told a reporter: "I used to dream about what a wonderful father he'd be."

Dwight Eisenhower: "Jimmy Stewart is among the greatest Americans."

Henry Fonda was one of Stewart's closest friends: "In the late sixties, we made a Western together called *Firecreek*. I was cast as the villain who tried to kill Jimmy. As soon as the movie was shown, I started getting loads of hate mail. Typical: 'You louse! How dare you try to shoot such a nice man? Shame!' The fans were right. It was unbelievable casting. How could anyone want to shoot Jimmy? He really likes people."

I had firsthand observation of that concern when some years ago I was in Hollywood writing a magazine article about him. Earlier, I had phoned my wife in Connecticut and learned that one of our daughters was running a high fever. We agreed that the child should be taken to the doctor. During the interview with Stewart, my wife called to report the pediatrician's findings: German measles.

Jimmy could see that I was very upset. "Don't worry, most children get it and soon are well," he assured me. "I think I had it myself when I was a kid." Then he grinned as he added, "Suppose that's what's wrong with me?"

That evening, he telephoned me at my hotel. He had checked with his doctor and learned that it is good for girls to get German measles when they are young. I can still remember his telling me in his deliberate, slow fashion: "See, that way she won't get it when she's married . . . and pregnant . . . and maybe bear a deformed child. See, it's all to the good."

I discovered that Stewart's guileless impact disarmed even the most cynical critic. It is composed of equal measures of strength, tenderness, innocent candor and chivalrous corn. A shy, hesitant person, he has a kindly drawl; is as honest as Kingdom Come; defies and defeats evil against heavy odds. The few times he has stepped out of character and played the heavy were box office duds.

These were some of Jimmy's greatest roles, with the lanky, stammering actor essentially playing himself—Mr. Small Town, a man of integrity:

## *MR. SMITH GOES TO WASHINGTON*

Jefferson Smith (Stewart) is the chief of the Scoutlike Boy Rangers. Because of his exemplary, homespun virtues, he is highly trusted and admired—although considered somewhat gullible. A U.S. Senate vacancy occurs in his state. The political machine boss (Edward Arnold) and his partner-in-crime, the senior senator (Claude Rains), agree that Smith would make the ideal puppet-appointee to cover up wide-scale graft. At stake is control of the state's industries, newspapers and radio stations.

Arriving in Washington, Smith is awed by the historic monuments and landmarks. The press hoots at his naiveté and earnest expressions of patriotism. When he refuses to engage in corrupt wheeling and dealing and pork barreling, he is framed on misconduct charges. His hard-boiled secretary (Jean Arthur) insists that he fight. When the Senate votes on his expulsion, he takes the floor in his own defense and filibusters for twenty-three hours. He succeeds in exposing the political venality in his home state. Smith is cleared before a cheering gallery, his strong faith in democracy confirmed.

## *HARVEY*

Elwood P. Dowd (Stewart) is a gentle, good-spirited, usually slightly inebriated philosopher who enjoys amusing friends. His closest companion is an imaginary six-foot white rabbit he calls Harvey. He carries on involved and profound conversations with the long-eared animal. Dowd's sister (Josephine Hull) frets about her brother's sanity. She wonders whether he should be committed to a mental hospital.

In the course of the movie, she and Dr. C. L. Chumley, a psychiatrist, come to realize that it would be a sad mistake to have Dowd turned into a conventional human being. They are overwhelmed by his practical wisdom: "I have wrestled with reality for forty years and I am happy to state that I have finally won out over it."

## IT'S A WONDERFUL LIFE

George Bailey (Stewart) runs a small building-and-loan company in upstate New York. He has a pretty, devoted wife, four wholesome children and a comfortable but shabby home. He is well-liked by the people in Bedford Falls, New York. An exception is miserly Jonathan Potter (Lionel Barrymore), president of the local bank. Potter high-pressures state examiners into scrutinizing Bailey's account books. They discover all the assets are missing—Bailey's assistant (Thomas Mitchell) has misplaced the funds.

Bailey feels that he has been a complete failure and that his entire life has been wasted. He gets drunk and wishes he had never been born. His guardian angel (Henry Travers) grants his wish. He shows him how empty Bedford Falls would be without him. Bailey is finally convinced how much he is loved and valued. He returns home in time to witness his multitudes of friends rally 'round with all the needed money.

## DESTRY RIDES AGAIN

The town of Bottle Neck in the wild, wild West is filled with outlaws. It is controlled by the owner of the Last Chance Saloon (Brian Donlevy) and Frenchy, a heavily painted dance hall girl (Marlene Dietrich). Together, they mastermind robberies and crooked poker games. In rides Deputy Tom Destry (Stewart), the son of a famous lawman who was killed defending law and order.

Young Destry's job is to clean up the town. But unlike his dead parent, he arrives minus guns. He believes that brains, not a fast draw, work best. However, when a friend is killed, he straps on his father's six-guns. Aided by Bottle Neck's decent citizens, he saves the town. He narrowly escapes death when Frenchy, who really has a heart of gold, steps in front of a bullet that was intended for him.

Again, goodness triumphs.

My warm thanks to the many men and women who shared their memories with me. Special appreciation to my wife, Sallie Prugh, for her everlasting help; Maurice Zolotow, who remains the most knowledgeable Hollywood hand; June Reno, for her skillful editing; Brenda Cahill and David Jacobson, whose research aided me tremendously; Anne Angelo, for typing the final manuscript; Bill Moorhead and the other fortunate residents of the actor's birthplace, Indiana, Pennsylvania. I agree wholeheartedly with Jimmy's recent comment: "That town is what America is all about."

So is Jimmy Stewart!


JHAN ROBBINS
*Columbia, South Carolina*

# CHAPTER I

# SMALL TOWN, U.S.A.

"We used to take our sidewalks in at night," said a former mayor of Indiana, Pennsylvania, the country town James Maitland Stewart was born in on May 20, 1908. "And that one-horse feeling has never left him. He has always stayed in touch—a small-town person with love of plain good things. He still drools over my Aunt Emma's peach pie and strawberry jam. I'm sure that he would really have rather stayed home."

Indiana, Pennsylvania (present population 16,000—it was 5,000 when Jimmy was born), is a set right out of an old Stewart movie: overtly patriotic, friendly, financially stable. "You people are living proof that American virtue still exists," observed the gangling, slow-speaking actor as he watched the local residents dedicate a nine-foot bronze statue of him on his seventy-fifth birthday. "This is where I sort of made up my mind about hard work being worth it, about community spirit, about the importance of a family, about the importance of God and the church." He blushed as he added, "I guess you should get the credit for making me what I am—that's if you're not too ashamed of admitting it. Waal, anyway, thanks from the bottom of my heart!"

The movie star and the town he was born in both have experienced changes. Stewart now has white hair, wears bifocals and a hearing aid. Indiana, Pennsylvania, has multistory buildings, a Burger King and stop lights. Yet much has remained the same. Jimmy still stammers, says "Aw, shucks," scratches his left ear with his right hand. Indiana, Pennsylvania, youngsters still hunt for frogs in Two Lick Creek, soap windows on Halloween, wave flags every July fourth.

The town is only an hour's drive from Pittsburgh but appears to be part of a more relaxed era, removed from time by a hundred years. It is nestled in the rolling hills of the Allegheny Mountains. Indiana, Pennsylvania, has numerous houses of Victorian design with gingerbread decor, a covered bridge, tree-lined streets and forty-one places of worship. "It's the way all of America should be like," Jimmy loves to exclaim. "Open and friendly."

It was originally an agricultural community. Now much of the farm acreage has gone to pine trees. Stewart's part of Indiana calls itself the "Christmas Tree Capital of the World." Fortunately, the town wasn't too caught up in the economic coal-is-king collapse that affected neighboring regions. It was economically diverse. Although some of the residents were engaged in getting coal out of the ground, many were farmers or employed at the local university or in factories that manufacture surgical equipment and rubber tires. They speak with pride of I.U.P.— Indiana University of Pennsylvania. Founded in 1875 as a state normal school, it now occupies ninety-eight acres and is only several blocks from the center of town.

"Indiana was saved by slow decisions and wisdom and the lack of greed," said Bill Moorhead, Jimmy's childhood friend. "None of his relatives still live here. Most of them are dead, but their influence is still keenly felt. I remember my father telling me, 'Those Stewarts always think before speaking. And what they say makes darn good sense!'"

Moorhead was I.U.P.'s assistant business manager until his retirement. He now collects bells that have historical significance. He has hundreds, including several that heralded the end of armed conflicts. "Jim kept ringing them on his last visit," Moorhead said. "His great-great-grandfather fought in the Revolutionary War. Since then there has been a Stewart in every American

15

war. It didn't matter if they were underweight or overage—somehow they managed to find ways to serve their country. Alexander Stewart, Jim's father, was forty-six when he went off to fight Germans in World War I. He had already been in the Spanish–American War. I suppose it's unusual for a small-town hardware store owner to be a Princeton graduate. But Alex was all that. He may have been considered a bit erratic, but he was always square on his feet. He knew where he was going. You believed him when he said he didn't want any 'high falutin' living.' Jim got many of his ideas straight from his father. Those two were always extremely close."

When Alexander Stewart was sent overseas, Jimmy made his mother buy him a miniature army uniform. "He wore it constantly," she said. "Refused to let me wash it. He was the most patriotic boy in town; wrote and produced two plays that were presented in our basement: *The Slacker* and *To Hell with the Kaiser*."

Another of Jimmy's boyhood companions, D. Hall Blair, recalled, "The Stewarts lived on Vinegar Hill, just a few streets from here. They had a big, rambling house with high ceilings. The front porch was filled with wicker furniture. We'd sit around, and Alex would tell us stories about his college days. There was a large piano in the parlor where we used to have songfests. Jim would play the accordion, his sister Virginia, the piano, and his sister Mary, the violin. They were both younger.

"Their parents often joined in the singing. They had good voices—especially Jim's mother. She was a very dignified lady—a strong churchgoer. Mrs. Stewart had finished college and would talk to us about the value of a good education. Jim often said he wished he had inherited her brains. He did inherit or adopt her slow, deliberate manner of speaking. Jim's father was garrulous by contrast.

"When reporters tried to interview Alex about his famous movie star son, he'd mischievously tell them, 'You've got the wrong guy. Follow me and I'll take you to Mr. Stewart.' He'd lead them to the back room of the hardware store on Indiana's Philadelphia Street. There, by the potbellied stove, the handyman-janitor was usually fast asleep. 'That's old man Stewart,' Alex would whisper. 'He's a very sad case. We try not to disturb him.' "

"When the reporters eventually discovered Alex's true identity," Blair said, "They'd want to write about him instead of Jim. He had fun playing with the press. If Alex had been on the stage, I'm sure he would have been a leading actor."

He was once described as follows by the Chamber of Commerce: "Alexander M. Stewart not only has a college degree from Princeton but is a very unusual businessman who often takes all kinds of odd items in place of cash. His store is a veritable museum."

It was more than that. A traveling sideshow that went broke traded its twelve-foot python to Alex for a hacksaw, a glass cutter and a toilet plunger. He put the snake in his store window. Jimmy, then seven years old, was charged with feeding it. One of the onlookers, a middle-aged spinster schoolteacher, swooned as she watched the youngster offer the python fat, wiggling mice he had caught in the store basement. She then tried to sue Alex for "threatening her life and limb." The charge was dismissed when Alex agreed to remove the snake.

"Late on a Sunday," Jimmy recalled, "Dad and his buddy, Dr. Torrance, went to the store and chloroformed the snake. For years it was a well-kept secret that they almost chloroformed themselves in the process. The snake eventually wound up in a zoo."

Everett McNair, a local farmer, needed several pounds of tenpenny nails to repair his barn. He offered in payment a battered accordion. Jimmy's father accepted. His wife, Elizabeth, who played the organ in the Presbyterian church they regularly attended, often said their young son needed a musical instrument so he could be introduced to spiritual music. With the help of the town barber, Jimmy learned the accordion quickly. His first tune was "O Sole Mio," a passionate Italian love song. He progressed to "God of Our Fathers," but the accordion was never admitted to church service.

The hardware store was filled with articles Alex had recklessly taken in trade. There was a German helmet, silver loving cups, a music box that played the final, belly-splitting aria of *Madam Butterfly*, Currier and Ives lithographs. (Alex once sent Jimmy a Currier and Ives print of the death of Andrew Jackson with Abraham Lincoln at his bedside. "Dad wanted me to hang it in the living room," Jimmy said. "I had to return the picture because it scared away all my dates.")

Alex was about to exchange a set of graded wrenches for a suit of Spanish armor when his wife, who was usually a sweet-tempered and reasonable woman, put her foot down. "Stop!" she shouted. "You already have enough junk to open your own yard!" He canceled that trade. Several days later, he acquired a porcelain figurine that he was told had once belonged to the King of Prussia. "And the man I got it from," Alex said excitedly, "only wanted two pounds of wood screws, a stew pot and twenty feet of screening. I sure got a bargain!"

In addition to the elaborate swap items he had collected, the store was filled with conventional hardware items. Alex just couldn't say no to a salesman. Abraham Jarvis, who described himself as a "once-was paint drummer," recalled, "Alex Stewart learned that all of my kids had come down with diphtheria. To help me out, he ordered four dozen gallons of white paint. I got an even bigger order when he heard that my wife needed a kidney operation. His store was such a warmhearted place, a kind of credit heaven."

"My earliest acute memories are of hardware smells," said Jimmy. "The dry aroma of coiled rope. The sweet smell of linseed oil and baseball gloves. The acid tang of open nail kegs. When I open my nose, they all come back to me."

"The Stewart family was knit close," said Bill Moorhead. "It was pretty apparent to everyone in town that they all liked each other. However, I think that Mr. Stewart was slightly partial to his son—he so wanted him to go into the hardware store. Alex was pleased by Jim's movie success, but he never really believed in it. Long after he should have retired, he kept the store going so that his son would have some 'real' kind of work to come back to when the 'screen stuff' was finished. I think that Alex was still waiting and hoping when he died at age eighty-nine."

"Jimmy had a straight, small-town upbringing," said Frank Moore, a prominent Indiana citizen and originator of Stewart's seventy-fifth birthday celebration. "He did many of the things Tom Sawyer was supposed to have done—perhaps more of them."

When he was four years old, Jimmy tied a box kite to his pushmobile and slid down the roof of his house. A stiff wind lifted the lean-fleshed youngster up in the air. He sailed several yards before landing in his father's arms.

A few years later he received an elaborate chemistry set for a birthday present. An ecstatic Jimmy immediately conducted a series of creative experiments, culminating with the manufacture of a giant stink bomb. His bedroom was so foul-smelling that he pleaded with his mother to be allowed to sleep on the porch. Elizabeth Stewart had the reputation of being a mild disciplinarian. This time she refused to grant permission. That night, a very miserable Jimmy slept with a wet washcloth on his nose to ward off the stench he had produced. His classmates urged him to make a similar bomb for school. Stewart was tempted, but the smell was still hanging in his bedroom. He declined.

"Jimmy was a much better student in science-related subjects than in the 3 Rs," one of his teachers said. "Spelling and proper pronunciation were never his specialities. He came up with the most original combinations of letters."

The drawls that later made Stewart famous in Hollywood amused his classmates. He was once asked to tell the class about a patriotic pageant he had listened to on the radio. "It was a hundred percent American show," he said. "It started off with the band playing 'The Germ of the Ocean.' "

Another time he noticed a leaky faucet in the home of the Blairs. "You gonna fix that fossip?" he wanted to know.

"What did you call it?" Hall Blair asked. "Spell it."

"F-o-s-s-i-p."

"No, it's faucet. F-a-u-c-e-t!"

"Isn't that what I just said? Fix the fossip!"

19

At home, Jimmy was assigned to weed pulling. His father ordered his ten-year-old son to rid the lawn of crabgrass, ragweed, dandelions and other undesirables. Jimmy had read *Tom Sawyer*. Apparently, his neighborhood friends had not. "The boy that gathers the most weeds will be declared the weed champion," he told them. Half a dozen local boys happily entered the contest. Soon the Stewart lawn and vegetable patch were weedless, and the town had a weed champion.

At school Jimmy organized a lunch-swapping club, as the peanut butter and jelly sandwiches his mother prepared for him were boring. He suggested the students trade lunch boxes. Stewart was soon enjoying hard-boiled eggs, ham sandwiches, jellied apples and chocolate cupcakes—his friends feasted on peanut butter sandwiches, which they were told were something special.

The future actor got an after-school job in the local movie theater. He helped operate the hand-cranked projector, rewound the film and set out the carbon arc lamps. Everything went well until he was asked to place a blue slide in front of the projector for the underwater scenes in *20,000 Leagues Under the Sea*. In his haste, Jimmy grabbed an orange slide. He was soon looking for another position.

"Alex gave him odd jobs around the store so he could earn enough money to take an airplane ride," said Mrs. Stewart. "Jimmy had his first flight when he was eleven. A barnstorming pilot was giving people fifteen minute rides for ten dollars. The plane flew in and out of Ed Bennett's field south of town—it was really a cow pasture. I admit I was scared to death, but I let him go anyhow."

"They were pretty nice about it," Jimmy recalled. "Dad drove me out, but on the way he stopped the car so we could pick up the family doctor. 'Just in case,' he told me. It was very evident that my parents had tremendous faith in this new invention."

Jimmy has often said that his love of flying was as great or greater than his devotion to acting. "If I hadn't gone to Hollywood," he said, "I'm sure I would have become a flyer. The buzz of a high-flying plane has always set my body tingling. I used to keep scrapbooks of aviation pioneers like Nungesser and

Coli. One book was filled with every picture and account I could find on the life of Charles A. Lindbergh."

He closely followed the Lone Eagle's historic flight to Paris. Recuperating from scarlet fever, Jimmy was kept home from school. "I built a model of Lindbergh's plane, *The Spirit of St. Louis*," he recalled, "also a model of the Woolworth Building to represent the U.S. and the Eiffel Tower for France." His father helped him place them in opposite corners of the store window. In between the two structures, Jimmy drew large maps of Newfoundland and Ireland. He would get the latest Western Union releases from the local newspaper office across the street. Then he would dash back to the store and move his model airplane closer to France.

"When Lindy's plane landed in Paris," Jimmy said, "Indiana went wild. Church bells rang. Everybody hugged. Grown women wept, laughed, kissed. It was better than New Year's Eve."

Another of Stewart's early projects was trying to construct crystal radio sets in empty oatmeal boxes. He was unsuccessful in his first attempts, but the stubborn perseverance he effectively demonstrated in his films was an essential part of his character. When he was eleven years old he built his first receiver that worked. He reported to Blair, "I actually got KDKA! And I'm three whole blocks away from the station!"

Several years later, he, Blair and another friend, Bill Neff, were building and selling homemade radios. They charged $20 for a one-tube set. "A local farmer was our most satisfied customer," Blair said. "He was able to get San Francisco and told his friends about it. We sold four more radios and had our picture taken by the *Gazette*."

Stewart and Neff decided to broaden into theater. The project: magic shows in the Stewart basement. They read a book about magic tricks. The two youngsters set a date, sold tickets, donned matching plus fours and argyle socks. Without rehearsal, they carefully placed Mary Stewart, Jimmy's seven-year-old sister, in a wooden box. It was covered with a white bed sheet. To the neighborhood audience, they announced they were going to saw her in half. They went about it.

21

When the blade approached the edge of the box, Mary jumped up and ran away screaming. Jimmy tried to placate the audience by playing his accordion and a musical saw. Years later, Neff became a professional magician and Stewart was made an honorary member of the American Society of Magicians, but he always remembered his initial attempt to mystify the public. "I guess maybe I don't blame Mary for mistrusting us," he said. "After all we could have severed her in two parts, but we meant no harm."

On August 2, 1923, President Warren G. Harding died. Several days later, the train carrying his body was scheduled to pass at 3:30 A.M. through a nearby town. Mrs. Stewart felt it was much too late for anyone to be up and out and said no when Jimmy asked to go. He was deeply disappointed and went to bed. At 2:30 A.M. he was awakened by his father. Pajamas under their outdoor pants, the two pushed the car out of the driveway. They arrived at the railroad station just as the black-draped, slow-moving train approached the platform. It was not scheduled to stop.

Jimmy's father shoved two pennies into his son's hand and shouted, "Quick, boy, run and put them on the rails!" The train passed over the coins; Jimmy dashed out and retrieved them. He returned one to his father and kept the other.

"For years," Jimmy said, "Dad and I carried those pennies flattened by the weight of history. And the knowledge that what was in my pocket was also in his made me feel very close to him and close to Indiana."

# CHAPTER II

# ARCHITECT OR ACTOR?

When Jimmy finished ninth grade, Alex decided that his only son should be sent away to a private boarding school. He chose Mercersburg Academy in Pennsylvania. Not only did it have a fine academic reputation, but it had been founded by Presbyterians and was still steeped in religion, with students attending chapel several times a week.

Although Alex had been told that enrollment was oversubscribed—that young Stewart couldn't possibly be accepted—he was insistent. "They should have known better," said Bill Hastings, news editor of the *Indiana Evening Gazette*. "Once Alex made up his mind about something, there was no way of stopping him. Nobody—but nobody—dared to contradict him!"

Mercersburg capitulated, and Jimmy became part of the class of '28. "I'm sure he enjoyed his stay," said Steve Brown, one of the actor's classmates. "He was pretty easygoing—much like he is today. However, his speaking style was even slower than it is now, if you can possibly imagine that. I remember when he tried out for varsity football. Why, it seemed that he didn't have strength enough to even finish a sentence, let alone charge a line. In his embarrassed, hesitant way, he asked, 'Is . . . this . . . the

. . . place . . . a . . . fella . . . gets . . . picked . . . for . . . the . . . football . . . squad?' Naturally, he was quickly rejected, but he did manage to become center for the Lightweight Team, which averaged about 120 pounds. We nicknamed him 'Elmer' because of his gawky, small-town qualities."

Stewart also sang in the Mercersburg choir, played accordion in the school orchestra and drew cartoons for the yearbook. In his final semester, he appeared in a melodrama about the French Revolution.

"A big sophomore named Angus Gordon was the narrator," Jimmy recalled. "His job was to tell the audience that there was going to be a fierce battle at midnight. He got so enthusiastic with the announcement that he took out his sword and brandished it around violently. Most of the props had been borrowed from local residents. As he swung it over an eighteenth-century table a lady in the audience screamed, 'Stop! That belongs to me!' But it was too late. Gordon had sliced the table in half. After that catastrophe, it was tough getting the audience back into the proper frame of mind."

Each summer, Stewart returned to Indiana to help out in the hardware store or to work at brick loading for a local building company. Ms. Addie Ross, Jimmy's next-door neighbor, said "Like everything else he did, he gave those jobs all his energy— never went at work halfway. On Sundays, he'd still go to church with his mother, who played the organ, and with his father, who sang in the choir. He was still active in the Boy Scouts. He had a stamp collection. Sounds corny, but that's exactly the way it was. Jimmy was always the most steadfast boy I've ever known, as well as being the most unpretentious." She smiled as she added, "He must have gotten his modesty from his mother. Alex certainly didn't have any to spare."

The Naval Academy in Annapolis was Jimmy's first choice for college. Again, his father had different thoughts. Since he had gone to Princeton, he felt that his son should follow in his footsteps. He had many fond memories, one of which being how he had masterminded the removal of the clapper from the bell that summoned students to class. He figured that without a bell to ring, classes would have to be suspended. He still had part of the clapper, which was displayed in the store window.

Another time, Alex and some fellow conspirators carried a cow up to the top of Princeton's Nassau Hall. "With a college education," he explained, "it's sure to give better milk!" Alex became a school legend. On Jimmy's first day at school, the proctor of his dormitory warned, "My father knew your father when he was here! I'm going to keep a sharp eye on you!"

Alexander Stewart's roommate at Princeton now taught one of the future actor's courses. "I didn't bother to study," Jimmy said. "I figured that because of his friendship with my father, he'd surely give me a high grade. I was in for a rude shock. At the end of the term he sadly told me, 'Young man, I've given you every possible help, but it's been to no avail!'"

Jimmy's major was civil engineering. He rapidly switched fields when another professor said, "Stewart, you do not have the slightest aptitude for engineering! I strongly suggest that you try something else!"

Teachers had always admired Stewart's drawing ability. He wondered if transferring to architecture would be a good idea. "After several nights of hard thinking," Jimmy said, "I resolved to become a second Frank Lloyd Wright. It turned out to be a wise move. I liked it and began to study. My grades improved. I felt better all over. Even started taking an interest in the way I looked—matching socks and shoes without holes."

Sal Lombardi, who had once owned a shoe repair shop in Princeton, New Jersey, recalled a visit young Stewart made to his store: "It was back in 1930. I remember the date because I just got my final citizenship papers. It was also in the middle of Herbert Hoover's term of office, and everybody was making jokes about him. Some smarty-pants townies came in for shines. They started up on Hoover. How he looked just like a stuffed pig. So I told them it wasn't right to speak that way about the President of the United States. That I was proud to have just become a citizen of this marvelous country. That's when they started up on me. They called me all kind of names—dago and wop. They wound up by saying, 'What does that guinea shoemaker know anyway?'

"Jimmy Stewart listened to all this. He had come in for soles and heels. He had been in the store before—was a nice, quiet customer who always asked me how I was. This time, however, what they said seemed to make him wild. He raised his fist and yelled, 'Apologize or I'll . . .' He never finished what he started to say. They ran out of the store like a mad bull was chasing after them. I was so grateful that I wanted to fix Jimmy's shoes for nothing. He just put out his hand. 'Welcome,' he told me. 'I'm real glad you're now part of the United States of America. Don't ever think that we're all like that!' "

Stewart now had time for extracurricular activities. He became a cheerleader and tried out for Princeton's famed Triangle Club. The acting group had been founded by novelist Booth Tarkington in 1881 and was considered one of the school's most prestigious organizations.

"When I went down to audition," Jimmy said, "I was dressed in a devil's costume complete with a long tail. I wore a mask and blew on a tin horn. The director kept shouting, 'Louder! And with more emotion!' It was real bedlam. I'm sure the reason I was selected was because they were hard up for talent."

Dr. Lila Cavanaugh, a prominent Boston pediatrician, was thirteen years old when she was taken to see one of the Triangle shows. "Jimmy sang and danced," she recalled. "The reason I particularly remembered him so vividly was because he appeared to be having such a good time while everyone else was trying too hard. After the performance, I went backstage to see my brother, who was also in the play. He introduced me to Jimmy. I complimented him on his dancing. 'That's good to hear,' he said. 'My mother keeps telling me that I have two left feet. I can't wait to tell her what you just said.' "

The student–architect–actor appeared in three Triangle plays:

*The Golden Dog, Spanish Blades* and *The Tiger Smiles.* Joshua Logan, now a very successful Broadway director and producer, was a fellow performer. "Our bumbling boy not only got a B.S. when he graduated," Logan said. "But also an A.B.—'Acting Bug.' He genuinely liked being on the stage, but it took him a long while to admit it—even to himself. In one of the Triangle plays I had written a part especially for him. He was very good. So much so that I asked him if he had ever thought of becoming an actor. 'Good God, no!' he shouted. 'I'm going to be an architect!' He bounced away as if I had just slapped him in the face with a wet fish. But I could tell that greasepaint and floodlights had hooked him.

"A few months later I became affiliated with a summer acting troupe known as the University Players, in Falmouth, Massachusetts. Some of the other members were Henry Fonda, Margaret Sullavan, Kent Smith, Mildred Natwick and Myron McCormick. I kept thinking about Stewart and sent him a wire to join us. He accepted. The rest is history."

"It sure wasn't that simple," Jimmy said. "You've got to remember that I graduated from Princeton in 1932—the depth of the Depression. Jobs were hard to come by. I figured that there wouldn't be any harm spending the summer on Cape Cod before going to graduate school or pounding on doors of architectural firms.

"I started out playing my accordion in the tearoom that was attached to the theater. That the customers weren't too appreciative is putting it mildly—they were downright hostile. More than one told me to shut up. Several disgruntled diners complained to the manager that my playing gave them upset stomachs. I was fired but hung around the theater sweeping floors, working on the props and painting scenery. I guess they got used to my being there and cast me in a play."

The University Players had an amazing influence on Broadway. It was not uncommon to see scouts from New York theaters in the audience. In rapid order, Stewart appeared in *Goodbye Again* and *Carry Nation*. He had four roles in *Carry Nation:* a constable, a member of a vigilante committee, an innocent by-stander and a colored gardener. "I didn't have the remotest idea that I was going to become a professional actor," Jimmy said. "I suppose I was just swept up in a crowd that was starting out in the theater and having a lot of fun. Before I knew it I was one of them. Acting for me was like being bitten by a malaria mosquito."

# CHAPTER III

# "GEE WHIZ, IS THIS REALLY BROADWAY?"

A New York drama critic saw Stewart in *Goodbye Again*. Although Jimmy had only a few lines: "Won't you please give him this book?" and "She's going to be sore as heck," the reviewer was very impressed. He wrote, "This play may soon come to our city . . . James Stewart who plays the chauffeur should come along. He seems to be Broadway material."

Jimmy wondered if he should try his luck on the New York stage. He asked Josh Logan what he thought. "If I were you," Logan replied with a straight face, "I'd shoot myself!" But when he noticed his friend's pained reaction, he quickly added, "I was only jesting. I've told you before that you're good—damn good! Yes, go to Broadway and become a full-fledged actor!"

"Okay," Jimmy replied. "I guess I'll give it a whirl."

He returned briefly to Indiana, Pennsylvania, to tell his parents about his decision to abandon architecture. 'They weren't too pleased," Stewart said. "I told them it was something I really wanted to try. Mother, bless her heart, said she'd back me up. Dad was upset. He kept shaking his head. 'No Stewart has ever gone into show business,' he said. Then he lowered his voice and whispered, 'Except one who ran off with a circus. And you know what happened to him? He wound up in jail!' "

* * *

Jimmy's initial Broadway appearance was in *Carrie Nation,* which had been hugely successful in Falmouth. In New York, however, it closed after a dismal run. Stewart's salary wasn't nearly sufficient to pay for his seventy-five dollar initiation fee to Actor's Equity. Fortunately, he was soon hired for *Goodbye Again,* another play he had done in summer stock.

The male lead was played by veteran actor Osgood Perkins, whose technique Jimmy admired. "His every move was dramatically significant," Stewart said. "There was a saying in show business: 'If you have a sick play on your hands, cast for Osgood Perkins. He'll prop it up!' "

George Haight, the play's co-author, recalled Stewart's fascination with Perkins. "He'd watch his every move, his every mannerism. It got to be a joke the way Jimmy idolized that man. If Osgood nodded his head in one direction, you could be sure that Jimmy would soon do the same. If Osgood waved his hands, Jimmy would adopt the gesture. I remember once during rehearsal this caused a bit of a stir. Osgood raised his hand the way kids do at school. He merely wanted to take a brief recess to relieve himself. Sure enough, Jimmy's hand shot up, too. He hid his face when Osgood headed for the bathroom."

*Goodbye Again* ran for nine months. When it closed, Stewart took a temporary job as an assistant stage manager. His first official assignment was to find a furry white cat that possessed a musical meow. After much searching, he located one in a back alley. However, her boyfriend, a large tomcat, insisted on coming along.

Although the audience cheered the cats when they made a brief appearance during the first act, they didn't much like the show. After a brief run it posted a final notice. Jimmy returned to acting. "I managed to get a few bit parts," he said. "But all in plays that closed before opening. My savings grew slimmer and slimmer. I was lucky that you could still get a blue plate special for well under fifty cents."

Richard Maney, one of Broadway's best-known publicists, worked on several plays Stewart appeared in. "That human skeleton," Maney said, "always looked hungry. I used to worry that he'd faint before the final curtain came down. In one of the shows he acted in—I believe it was *Spring in Autumn*—he had to play the concertina. I half expected him to keel over from malnutrition before he finished the melody."

In the summer of 1933, Stewart was hired by a company that played in a Long Island, New York, barn theater. His role was that of a deranged airplane pilot. "The plot was real zany," said Seth Sayer, a fellow performer. "Most of the action took place aboard the plane. I was one of the passengers. The lot of us, including the pilot, were contemplating mass suicide. I'm sure the audience wished we had followed through.

"Everything about the play was clear-cut. The director wanted us to be certain that we finished the first act before 8:57. 'Remember!' he ordered, 'Before 8:57!' I recall Jimmy saying that the director must have a hang-up about that number—'Maybe he was born at that time or it was when his wife walked out on him.' We soon found out why he was so demanding—a freight train passed right next to the barn at exactly 8:57!"

Acting jobs were hard to come by in the 1933–34 season. Again, Stewart turned to stage managing. He got a job with a touring company. This time he was instructed to see to it that Jane Cowl was satisfied with her starring role in *Camille*. "I guess Miss Cowl wasn't too pleased with me," Jimmy said. "Maybe I sort of gave her some trying moments?"

That was an understatement. Once in Boston, when the actress was in the midst of the famous death scene, Stewart ran into the alley to investigate some strange noise. "I knew that the slightest sound upset her," Jimmy said. He found two vagrants arguing and managed to shoo them away. However, when he tried to reenter the theater, the back door was shut tight. He vigorously shoved and pulled. The resulting racket caused the temperamental actress to leave her deathbed and demand that the curtain be lowered. Then, still in a rage, she ordered the young assistant stage manager be fired.

Stewart's first important Broadway role was as the idealistic soldier–guinea pig in Sidney Kingsley's *Yellow Jack*. It was a dramatization of Walter Reed's fight against yellow fever. "I

31

almost missed out on that role because I didn't have an Irish accent," Stewart recalled. "The first time I tried out, they turned me down. Then I went around finding all the Irishmen I could. I must have listened to several dozen policemen and firemen. I listened to them day and night. When the trick seemed to be mine, I returned to the producer, and he gave me another chance. That time I stuck."

The drama critic of the *New York Sun* said, "James Stewart seems to have talent as well as scruples . . . The play deserves a long run."

Jimmy was sure that his next stage venture, *All Good Americans*, written by humorist S. J. Perelman, was also headed for a lengthy engagement. Audiences disagreed. It closed after a few performances. "I think that the theater constantly frustrates insiders," Stewart said. "Plays that you think are going to be sure hits turn out to be real clinkers. It's a topsy-turvy world. I suppose the reason is really simple: the writer, director, producer and actors are all too close to the play. They lose objectivity. They get immune to all the faults."

That, however, wasn't the case with *Journey by Night*, an Austrian play the Shuberts brought to Broadway. "From the very beginning I knew it was doomed," said Jimmy, "but I needed a job, and it did pay $55 a week."

Stewart was cast as the younger brother of a character played by Albert Dekker, a very successful and prosperous banker. He falls in love with Dekker's wife and embezzles bank funds so that he can run off with her. The police are alerted, and a desperate Stewart kills his lover and dumps her body in the Danube river.

"The plot was just awful," Jimmy said. "But as if that wasn't enough, I had a series of mishaps the two nights the show ran." Once again, Stewart had trouble with stuck doors. On opening night in Broadway's 44th Street Theater, he heard a loud knock in the middle of the second act. In response to his "Who's there?" he learned it was the travel agent who was bringing Stewart boat tickets so he and his paramour could flee the country.

Jimmy eagerly attempted to open the door. But it wouldn't budge. He tried harder. The chandeliers shook. Chairs fell over.

An end table capsized. The travel agent finally managed to enter through the bedroom.

The following night, Stewart stumbled against the living room wall, causing it to come tumbling down. The telephone began ringing when it wasn't supposed to. A frantic Jimmy kept answering: "I'm much too busy to talk now! I'll call back later!" He never got the chance—the play closed that night. A critic who reviewed the jinxed play wrote, "Stewart's as Viennese as hog and hominy."

While he was "at liberty"—the show business expression for out of work, Stewart and some of his friends, including Henry Fonda, Burgess Meredith, Myron McCormick, Josh Logan and Benny Goodman, organized what they called the Thursday Night Club. "Its predominant purpose," said McCormick, "was to play poker. But mostly we were broke and just kidded around. Jimmy loved to sing "Ragtime Cowboy Joe" and "Minnie from Mars." Sometimes, we'd play for imaginary stakes." Shortly before his death, McCormick said, "I think he still owes me $3 million!"

## CHAPTER IV

# "MOVIES NEED SOMEONE AS CLEAN AND SINCERE AS YOU"

"I am responsible for Jimmy coming to movieland," said Hedda Hopper, the actress and Hollywood gossip columnist. "It happened when the two of us were appearing in a show called *Divided by Three*. Guthrie McClintic was the producer; Judith Anderson had the leading part of an affection-split woman who loves her lover, her husband and her son; Jimmy was the son. During a dress rehearsal in New Haven, it became evident that Stewart's acting would win the sympathy of the audience, and he'd steal all the notices. Judith was worried. She insisted that Guthrie do something. He decided to rewrite the second act."

The new material called for Jimmy to bring home his fiancée to meet his parents and the family's best friend. For the first time, Stewart was to learn that the best friend was also his mother's paramour. With his betrothed on stage, he was to turn and call his mother a whore. When the producer sprang the new line, Jimmy fell apart. He begged to be let out of the play. "I can't possibly do that, Mr. McClintic! Under no circumstance could I bring myself to call any woman that—and my mother! Especially with the girl I intend to marry standing beside me!"

"Guthrie reminded him that he had a contract," Hedda said. "The line stayed in. At the end of the rehearsal, Jimmy looked

34

so depressed that I told him, 'The screen needs a young man as clean and sincere as you. Why aren't you in Hollywood?'

" 'For what?'

" 'Pictures of course.'

"He laughed in that embarrassed way of his, saying ruefully, 'Waal, what would they do with this puss of mine? I'm no Arrow collar ad.'

" 'You're an actor,' I said. 'They could fix that. Pictures desperately need someone like you. You project sincerity.' Again, Jimmy laughed it off, but he looked less tense. I could tell that I had planted a seed. A short time later, I introduced him to Al Altman, who was in charge of eastern recruiting for a major studio."

Altman arranged for a photographic test. His instruction terrified the young stage actor who later said, "I couldn't tell if he was off his rocker or I was or both."

"Now, Stewart," the Hollywood recruiter commanded. "Imagine that I have a large horse in the palm of my right hand. I'm going to release him so that he can gallop up to you. He goes obediently, but the path he chooses is to go up the wall, across the ceiling and down the other wall. After that he will come back to me and climb into my hand."

Jimmy was puzzled but agreed to take the test. "I never learned the results," he said. "I tried to convince myself that it was just as well. If this was a sample of Hollywood, I was better off on Broadway. But the truth is that my pride was hurt."

A few months later, he was rediscovered. This time by Bill Grady, a talent scout for Metro-Goldwyn-Mayer. He had seen Stewart in several shows and was impressed. "I like this kid," he told his bosses. "Unaffected, decent." Jimmy was summoned to Hollywood.

Although he had long been one of the air industry's greatest boosters, he arrived in California by train. His luggage included a mysterious black case that looked as if it contained a submachine gun. When a Pullman porter tried to pry it away, Jimmy warned, "Don't! The slightest jolt will cause big trouble!"

Stewart recalled, "I didn't let it out of my sight for a single moment. It was quite a trick sleeping with it in an upper berth. I sure was thankful when we finally reached Pasadena."

The black case contained a present for Henry Fonda, who had preceded him to the movie capital. When Jimmy's train pulled into the station, he was met by his friend. Stewart handed him the case. Inside was a model of an airplane—a copy of a Martin Bomber the two had built when they had roomed together in New York City.

MGM wasn't impressed. Unenthusiastically, they signed Jimmy to a contract at minimum wage. It was for seven years, renewable every six months, starting at $350 a week. Henry Rapf, a studio producer, was told to make some use of the new property. His first words to Stewart were, "My God, you're skinny!" He ordered him to visit the studio's in-house body builder, Don Loomis.

"Do they think I'm a magician?" said Loomis as he stared at Jimmy. He finally asked him, "What's your height?"

"Six-three-and-a-half."

"Weight?"

"One hundred and thirty."

"You're beyond helping!"

"Please try! I'll cooperate! I promise!"

"Okay! Okay! But I don't *promise* anything! Let's start by you picking up that barbell."

Jimmy groaned a few times and managed to heave it to his waist. Loomis looked disgusted. "I just had a little kid hoist it over his head a dozen times!" he snapped. "Can't you do anything?"

The body builder worked with Stewart four days a week. In addition, he recommended that Jimmy drink milkshakes and eat banana splits topped with whipped cream. "I doubt it, but maybe, maybe they'll put some fat on your ribs," he said grimly.

"I had dozens of them," Stewart recalled. "I was lucky that at the time they cost less than a dime apiece. But even then it took a big chunk out of my budget. I hadn't received my first paycheck yet.

"Hank Fonda also helped me gain some weight. He, too, was

very skinny, and someone had told him that milk mixed with brandy was a very good way to add pounds. We started with a lot of milk and a little bit of brandy. But Hank felt that we should add more brandy. Then some more. Soon the color got darker and darker. We used to drink that concoction for breakfast and by 8 A.M. we were half stoned. Anyway, I gained some weight."

When Rapf felt that Jimmy was more presentable-looking, he grudgingly agreed to cast him in a movie. Stewart's first screen appearance was as the trusted reporter pal of Spencer Tracy in *The Murder Man*—a quickie shot in three weeks. It was a mystery drama of which one reviewer wrote, "To call it bad, would be the improper use of the word! It assails the nostrils!"

Jimmy's name in the movie was Shorty, causing Rapf to remark, "I should have my head examined for giving him that part. I needed a midget. So what do I get? A human giraffe!"

The gangling actor, who was billed ninth, was very upset when he saw himself in the rushes. "I was all hands and feet," he said. "Didn't seem to know what to do with either. I wondered if I had made the right choice. Maybe I should have stuck to architecture?"

Several weeks later, Stewart was even more perplexed. He was tested for a part in Pearl S. Buck's *The Good Earth*. "I was to play the part of a Chinese man," Jimmy said. "They got the makeup department to design a special oriental mask for me. It took three hours to put on, but I felt it was worth it. I thought I really looked the part—even my own mother wouldn't recognize me.

"Proudly, I paraded around the studio lot showing off. But everyone I met said, 'Hello, Jimmy.' After all that, the director decided that I was much too tall. So what did he do? He had a trench built for me to walk in. Paul Muni, the star, walked beside me. P.S. I didn't get the part. It went to a real Chinese man who was five-foot-two!"

Shortly after that disappointment, Stewart was given another minor role, in *Rose Marie,* a movie operetta starring Jeanette MacDonald and Nelson Eddy. (The film featured the tremendously popular duet, "Indian Love Call.") Jimmy played the soprano's weak-willed brother who was hiding from the law in a deserted Canadian cabin. Royal Canadian Mountie Eddy tracked him down. Reluctantly, he slipped handcuffs on the protesting Stewart who kept insisting, "But I'm your sweetheart's brother!"

Margaret Sullavan, his good friend from the University Players, arranged for his next screen part. Her daughter, Brooke Hayward, told how it happened: "Mother wanted him to play opposite her in a movie she was to star in, *Next Time We Love*. With crossed fingers she said to the casting director, 'Why don't you try to get Jimmy Stewart for the male lead?'

" 'Who is Jimmy Stewart?'

" 'Why, just about the hottest property around town!'

" 'Never heard of him.'

" 'You will! He'll probably win an Oscar for his supporting role in *Rose Marie!*'

On Margaret Sullavan's warm recommendation, Universal borrowed Jimmy from MGM. Stewart played a foreign correspondent whose wife (Sullavan) refuses to accompany him to assignments in Rome and Moscow. She is a struggling actress who is determined to become a star. After an hour and a half of tears and pathos, the couple—and their baby—are reconciled. A reviewer for *Time* magazine wrote: "Stewart disregards a long established cinema convention for such roles, ably introduces to Hollywood the character of a newspaperman who is neither a drunkard, lecher nor buffoon."

Jimmy's fourth film was a major MGM production: *Wife Vs. Secretary*, in which Myrna Loy (wife) and Jean Harlow (secretary) fight over magazine publisher Clark Gable. Jimmy, the secretary's boyfriend, innocently comes between them. The script called for a kissing scene with Harlow, then known as "the platinum-haired sex queen" and the "blonde bombshell."

"I soon found out why she was called those names," Jimmy said. "Clarence Brown, the director, wasn't too pleased by the way I did the smooching. He made us repeat the scene about half a dozen times. I now have to confess that I botched it up on purpose. That Jean Harlow sure was a good kisser. I realized that until then I had never been really kissed!"

In 1936, Jimmy made *Small Town Girl* with Janet Gaynor and Robert Taylor. Although Taylor was the featured lead, many reviewers singled out "Jimmy Stewart, the screen's brightest discovery." In the film, one of his lines was, "Are you keeping your chin up?" It became a popular national slogan—more than a dozen newspapers included the question in their editorials.

Stewart appeared with Joan Crawford, Lionel Barrymore, Franchot Tone and Melvyn Douglas. He was selected by Cole Porter, then the country's leading composer of popular music, to be the leading man in *Born to Dance*. Jimmy played a shy enlisted navy man who meets a talented dancer (Eleanor Powell) in a lonely hearts club. They fall in and out of love. Stewart sings several Porter numbers. One critic wrote that it was reminiscent of "the hired man calling in the cows for supper. They come in with a smile, but they look rather surprised . . . Stewart is very much like the rest of us average guys. Only, our singing—like his—should be reserved for the shower. However, one of the songs is quite catchy. It's called, 'I've Got You Under My Skin.' "

The MGM publicity department began releasing stories about Jimmy Stewart, "The upright average man . . . product of a small American town and God-fearing parents . . . endowed with a keen sense of humor."

One handout claimed that "The stuttering boy-next-door isn't very concerned with sartorial matters. He is much happier in a beat-up windbreaker than a three-piece business suit." It told of a fan from Little Rock, Arkansas, who wrote, "Jimmy, your face and clothes look as if they have been lived in. I like them that way. Stay like the rest of us. Don't ever change!"

# CHAPTER V

# BETTER AND BETTER

Lee Sheffield, now retired, was a cameraman on several of Jimmy's early movies. "The common decency of the guy was always showing up," he said. "I remember Woody [W. S.] Van Dyke, who directed him in *After the Thin Man*, saying, 'It's a pleasure to work with Stewart—he isn't above himself like the other actors. You can almost touch his goodness.'

"Woody's opinion was shared by the rest of the crew. One time, after a long, often repeated scene, I complained that it was damn hot—the lights were frying me. The next thing I knew, Jimmy handed me a tall glass of iced tea. He had overheard my griping and ran to get me one. Here he was directly behind William Powell and Myrna Loy in the billing, running errands like a fifth assistant cameraman! He shrugged off my thanks with that shy, lopsided twist of a shoulder that plainly said, 'Never mind, no trouble.' "

Gale Sondergaard, who appeared with Stewart in the 1937 remake of *Seventh Heaven,* had a similar recollection. "During the shooting, a bunch of elementary school children were permitted to visit the set. Their teacher warned them to keep very still, but a fresh-faced boy of about six started pushing the kid next to him. Gregory Ratoff was in the middle of a scene when it happened. He walked over menacingly. Jimmy, who had the leading role of a Paris sewer cleaner, stepped in between them.

"Simone Simon, who had the other leading part, was standing close by. During the lunch break she told me what Jimmy had said to the boy. 'It helps me a whole lot when you're quiet, otherwise I might blow my lines. Besides, it gets mighty cold in the next scene and your words might freeze to your face. Now, you wouldn't want that to happen.' Then he patted the youngster's head. After that the boy didn't make another sound."

Jimmy was rapidly progressing in his cinema career. A reviewer for the *New York Daily Mirror* wrote, "A couple of good things have come out of the depression, Jimmy Stewart for one thing. With each new movie he keeps getting better and better. He's the original perseverance kid."

That industriousness paid off. Jimmy was now either first or second in the listing of screen credits. Late in '37, he made a movie with Edward G. Robinson. Most critics called *The Last Gangster* ludicrous: Joe Krozac (Robinson), a powerful underworld czar, is sent to Alcatraz for income tax evasion. His wife (Rose Stradner) has just given birth. She divorces the gangster to protect the child from all the notoriety. Eventually, she marries Paul North (Stewart), a crusading reporter. When Krozac is released from prison, his former mob associates demand to know where he has secreted the money. He refuses to tell. Desperate, they kidnap his young son, hoping it will force him to reveal the hiding place. Krozac manages to get the boy back, but is fatally wounded. With his last breath, he begs North to promise that he will continue to be a good stepfather.

This time the reviewer for the *Daily Mirror* said, "Despite the hackneyed story, Jimmy, sporting a preposterous-looking mustache, manages to make it slightly credible. To call him a professional do-gooder sounds patronizing. He's a professional who happens to be good . . . He's the most important new discovery in Hollywood."

Jimmy sent the critic a warm thank-you note. He continued that practice throughout his career. Brendan Gill, of the *New Yorker* magazine, said, "Stewart is one of the few exceptions to

41

risk the age-old tabu against actors thanking a reviewer for a favorable review."

In the nineteenth-century drama *Of Human Hearts*, Jimmy plays a famous Civil War surgeon who forgets his early family roots. Rebelling against his stern, righteous preacher father, the Rev. Ethan Wilkins (Walter Huston), he runs off to medical school. After a dozen years of international fame and gracious living, he is reunited with his grieving widowed mother (Beulah Bondi) through the efforts of President Abraham Lincoln (John Carradine).

"Jimmy acted so natural," said Carradine, "that he had me thinking I was actually the Great Emancipator. He has the ability to make everything feel plausible. I even imagined that I was the author of the Gettysburg Address."

A short time later, Stewart was selected to play opposite Ginger Rogers in *Vivacious Lady*, a good-natured but belabored drawing-room comedy. RKO cast him as a timid assistant botany professor from a small midwestern college who is sent to New York to rescue a wayward cousin from the clutches of avaricious city slickers. Jimmy meets a sophisticated nightclub performer (Rogers). After a whirlwind courtship, the two opposites marry. The rest of the ninety-two minute movie is devoted to the tribulations of the new wife adjusting to academic life.

At an important end-of-term school dance, the professor awkwardly dances with a former girlfriend. As the couple stumble across the floor, his partner presses her body against his. "They're sure moving around mighty close," observes his mother.

"Close!" Ginger replies. "If they were any closer, she'd be behind him!" Jimmy starts to protest, but his stuttering gets him all twisted up. It became a national parlor game to imitate Stewart's slow walk and even slower drawl. Brooklyn's Loews Pitkin Theater ran a "Jimmy Stewart Sound-Alike Contest" in conjunction with his movie *You Can't Take It with You*.

Dozens of entrants shuffled across the stage drawling "Gee whiz" and "Aw, shucks." The winner was an unemployed plumber who pretended to be Stewart on a basketball court: Jimmy is about to toss in the winning point in the final ten seconds of the championship game when a player from the opposing team falls down. Instead of flipping the ball through the net, Stewart runs over to his disabled rival, picks him up and says, "Waal . . . winning isn't everything . . . sportsmanship is what really counts!"

Mischa Auer, who portrayed a sarcastic Russian ballet teacher in the movie, had been flown in from California to be the judge. He told the cheering audience, "That's exactly what Jimmy would do and say. He even worries that the prop man will get a hernia from carrying heavy trunks!"

*You Can't Take It with You* was adapted from a hugely successful zany Broadway stage play that was written by George S. Kaufman and Moss Hart. Frank Capra, the film's director, cast Jimmy as the lead—a very, very naive but very, very honest young man who believes in simple values. He disapproves of his father (Edward Arnold) conducting shady business; approves of his prospective grandfather-in-law (Lionel Barrymore) collecting staunch friends and canceled stamps. The movie was a great hit in London, where it ran for seven months.

The film critic of London's *New Statesman* wrote, "No actor on the screen today manages to appear more unconscious of script, camera and director than Mr. Stewart . . . Not only is Mr. Stewart unaffected but unbeatable."

Jimmy was recently asked if the film would stand a chance today. "I think it would," he replied. "Hollywood got its start by providing escapism entertainment, and that is what it still provides best."

Carole Lombard, who was regarded as one of Hollywood's superstars, was once the guest of honor at a dinner party given by Marion Davies. "After we finished coffee and a delicious meringue dessert," Lombard said, "we all played a guessing game about well-known people. The person who was up had to act out his selection's characteristics. It was Frank Capra's turn. Slowly, he ambled up and down the immense living room; lowered his head as if he was fearful of it coming off; put his arms in front of his face; grinned shyly; kept brushing hair out of his eyes.

" 'Jimmy Stewart!' I yelled.

"I was right. After the game, Frank kept singing Jimmy's praise. How he was a fine actor. How he was so easy to work with. How he didn't require caviar brought to his dressing room on a silver platter. A lot of things like that. I was so impressed I demanded that David [David O. Selznick had just signed Lombard for a starring role in *Made for Each Other*] get him for the male lead. He did. It was a very wise move. The movie was highly successful."

Most of the reviewers agreed with the *Newsweek* critic, who said, "Carole Lombard and Jimmy Stewart are perfectly cast in the leading roles . . . Together, they never allow the movie to get clumsy in its effective assault on the emotions."

They were less enthusiastic about Stewart's next two films: *Ice Follies of 1939* and *It's a Wonderful World*. Although his co-stars were Joan Crawford and Claudette Colbert, both movies drew extremely dismal notices. Crawford, who had her hair dyed jet black for the ill-fated role, said, "I have to admit I was graceless on ice, but you should have seen Jimmy!"

One of the unkindest reviews appeared in a Washington, D.C., newspaper: "Shakespeare's immortal line can only do justice to this mishmash, 'The rankest compound of villanous smell that ever offended nostril.' Putting Joan Crawford and Jimmy Stewart on skates is just as ridiculous as hanging a no-admittance sign on the entrance of a mine that Eleanor Roosevelt is determined to visit. It just won't wash!"

In the equally incredulous *It's a Wonderful World*, Stewart plays a sardonic, money-mad private eye. During an unbelieveable eighty-six minutes, he threatens Colbert, an aspiring poetess, speaks disparagingly of her rhymes and socks her on the jaw, all while wildly changing from one disguise to another. Frank Davis, the producer of the absurd farce, said, "The studio should have known that Jimmy Stewart would never do any of those unconvincing things. However, I predict that his next film, *Mr. Smith Goes to Washington*, will more than make up."

# CHAPTER VI

# MR. SMITH GOES TO WASHINGTON

Sidney Buchman, author of the screenplay *Mr. Smith Goes to Washington,* wondered what would happen if a decent, trusting person found himself by accident a legislator in the nation's capital. The now historic story was not written with Jimmy Stewart in mind. It happened in Columbia Pictures casting office quite casually late on a Friday afternoon. "How about this?" asked a junior staff member. "Why don't we get Jimmy Stewart for the title role?" After many story conferences, he was selected to play the naive, honest Senator Jefferson Smith. The rest is film history.

Critics, usually a hard-shell bunch, were carried away by his performance. *Newsweek:* "Stewart gives the most persuasive characterization of his career as a one man crusade against political corruption." *Baltimore Sun:* "The finest performance of the year." *Chicago Tribune:* "It should be must viewing for all legislators."

The foreign press was equally enthusiastic. France: "Provincial Washington urgently needs more lawmakers with the honor of Stewart." Italy: "Not only is Jimmy Stewart eloquent and expressive, but truly a noble artist. His concluding speech is pure poetry, proving that sometimes even deaf ears can hear." England: "James Stewart's Senator Jefferson Smith exposes rampant political intrigue so masterly. His characterization of an American senator should earn him Hollywood's highest award."

It was thought that Stewart would easily win an Oscar for the job. Betting handicappers rated him an eight-to-five favorite. When it was announced that Robert Donat, star of *Goodbye, Mr. Chips,* had won, a disappointed Jimmy said philosophically, "I guess there's always another year. This one sure produced some mighty stiff competition." (This included Donat, Clark Gable in *Gone With the Wind,* Laurence Olivier in *Wuthering Heights* and Mickey Rooney in *Babes in Arms.*)

For more than a decade, the Oscar had been the film industry's most coveted award. It was created to upgrade standards and to counter criticism from the vocal section of the population that came to be known as the Moral Majority. Throughout the twenties, influential church groups fiercely attacked the Hollywood life-style in and out of films. Although a censorship program administered by the "Hays Office" regulated cinema behavior (for example, in a bedroom scene, one actor must keep at least one foot on the floor) it was still common to hear the entire industry denounced from the pulpit. The Reverend Dr. C. Martin Baker, spokesman for Americans Concerned with Decency in the Movie Industry, was one of the chief assailants. "Sodom and Gomorrah were sweet-smelling places compared to the everyday goings-on in Hollywood!" he charged. "They are disgusting and viciously defiling!"

Respectability was needed: recognition of refinement in the art. Louis B. Mayer, who would be Jimmy's boss when he came to MGM, conceived the idea of giving pretentious public awards for outstanding moviemaking achievements. His colleagues liked the suggestion, and the newly formed Academy of Motion Picture Arts and Sciences agreed to sponsor what soon became a distinguished annual ceremony—presented, of course, Hollywood style.

Each year, Academy members are asked to select nominees from their own fields: acting, writing, directing and other categories connected to moviemaking. The leading candidates compete in a runoff. Again the Academy polls its membership. This time they are asked to select one name in each speciality. The three top classes are Best Picture, Best Actor and Best Actress. The ballots are carefully guarded by Price Waterhouse, an international accounting firm which verifies and totals the votes. The name of the winner in each classification is placed in a sealed envelope and not opened until the category is called at the gala award ceremony.

Millions of TV viewers watch the winners receive ten karat gold-plated statuettes weighing eight and a half pounds and measuring thirteen and a half inches in height. Its nickname derives from an observation of an Academy librarian. When she first saw the award, she gasped in surprise, "Why, it looks just like my Uncle Oscar!" It's been affectionately known as Oscar ever since. (Actress Bette Davis and Hollywood columnist Sidney Skolsky both have claimed credit for the name.)

When Jimmy failed to win an Oscar for *Mr. Smith,* many newspapers devoted more space to the losing candidate than to the winner. One of the more indignant stories appeared in the *New York Daily Mirror:* "Jimmy was gypped! It wasn't enough that he won the New York Critics Award hands down. Double nuts to England!" (Donat had played a British schoolmaster in the British-made *Goodbye, Mr. Chips.*)

Stewart's next movie, *Destry Rides Again,* also drew partisan comments. The *Mirror* reviewer was still angry. This time he said, "Jimmy Stewart keeps on being gypped. His performance as the peaceable lawman was also of Oscar caliber!"

Destry was a remake of an old Tom Mix western. Much of the action takes place in a rough-and-tumble saloon called Last Chance. The story line was very similar to *Mr. Smith Goes to Washington:* a naive good guy beats the evildoer.

Marlene Dietrich, who played a warm-hearted, cigar-smoking dancehall singer, was his co-star. At the end of the filming, the sultry German-born actress said, "I never enjoyed working in Hollywood as much as I did when I was working with Jimmy. He's *ein feganer Mensch*" (a sweet human being).

Jimmy took a great interest in the backstage crew in all of his pictures. Mike Chaffey, a retired studio electrician in the crew of *Destry,* recalled, "I had just returned to work after burying my wife. I figured that getting back would take my mind off her death. But I figured wrong. I was practically off my rocker from grief—and showed it.

"Jimmy heard about my mental outlook. A couple of times he stopped to talk to me in private. Didn't say much, just listened. Let me get my thoughts out loud. Boy, is that important! Once he had me meet him at the Brentwood Presbyterian Church. I understand he has since become an elder of that church. I'm not a bit surprised. There's no question that his taking an interest in me helped me to feel better."

Stewart has been a regular churchgoer most of his life. He didn't, however, attend services in California until his father came out to visit. Alexander Stewart wanted to know why his son had become a backslider.

"There isn't any Presbyterian church nearby."

"I'll investigate!"

An hour later, Alex returned with three men in tow. "They are elders in the Brentwood Presbyterian Church, which is just a few blocks north of here," he explained. "They said they were having trouble raising money for a new addition. That's when I told them that I had a son who is a famous movie star and makes lots of money. I promised your help."

Mike Chaffey, the studio electrician Jimmy had befriended, had other stories to demonstrate Stewart's moral principles. "There were lots of us he gave a leg up." Chaffey recalled. "One guy was called Specs because he wore heavy glasses and was always bumping into things. He took a lot of kidding and was used to being told he was so uncoordinated that he couldn't chew gum and blow his nose at the same time. Jimmy noticed what was happening. Purposely, he started taking pratfalls to take the sting off Specs. Loud and clear he'd say that ever since he was a kid he was the most awkward guy in the world—didn't know where he was putting his feet!

"Then there was this older guy we used to call Methuselah. He was only in his fifties, but he looked at least seventy. If you can imagine, he spoke even slower than Jimmy. And like him, he was always forgetting things. I remember Jimmy taking his side and telling us, 'I guess some people are slower than others. Me, for instance. My mental process has never been lightning fast. That's why I'm pretty terrible at card games. It takes me forever to memorize my lines. Why, sometimes I can't even remember my hat size!' "

In 1940 and '41, Jimmy starred in seven movies: *The Shop Around the Corner, The Mortal Storm, No Time for Comedy, The Philadelphia Story, Come Live With Me, Pot o' Gold* and *Ziegfeld Girl*. He was cast as a lonely Hungarian department store clerk, a Nazi-hating farmer, a successful playwright, a sardonic newspaper-man, a destitute young author, a zany harmonica virtuoso and a jilted suitor who turns the other cheek. He played opposite Margaret Sullavan, Rosalind Russell, Katharine Hepburn, Hedy Lamarr, Paulette Goddard, Lana Turner and Judy Garland.

His performance in *The Philadelphia Story* won him an Academy Award for Best Actor in 1940. Jimmy played a self-loathing reporter who is sent to Philadelphia to cover a high society wedding. Tracy Lord (Katharine Hepburn) is getting married for the second time. Her husband-to-be is a very rich and very stuffy coal company executive (John Howard). The bride's mother invites her former son-in-law (Cary Grant) to the festivities. To Hepburn, he reminisces about their honeymoon aboard a sloop called *True Love*. She tries to be nonchalant, to shrug the memory off, but in spite of herself, she responds wistfully with a line that has since become famous, indicating the quality of gameness: "My, she was so yar."

After downing several glasses of champagne, Hepburn begins to realize that a large part of the first marriage troubles were her fault—the fault of arrogance. Very late that night, she throws most of her clothes off and dives into the pool. Jimmy rescues her and innocently carries her back to the house. When Hepburn's prospective husband sees his near-nude fiancée in Stewart's arms, he departs in a hurry. But the wedding goes off on schedule—with a slight change of bridegroom: Cary Grant re-marries Katharine Hepburn.

Jimmy didn't get the girl, but he did win an Oscar, which he sent to his father for safekeeping. Alex promptly placed it in his hardware store window. Many fans thought the Oscar was by way of an apology for Stewart's failure to win the previous year.

"I guess it could be true that I won it as a deferred payment," Jimmy said. "Come to think of it, I've always felt that Bette Davis won an Oscar for *Jezebel* because she should have had it for *Of Human Bondage*. Other oversights, I suspect, have been made up this way. I suppose that's okay, since right usually triumphs eventually."

Although he has always been in great demand, Stewart is a natural worrier. "I've always been that way," he said. "When I was between pictures, I'd think that I had just made my last film. That no one in his right mind could possibly want me. I was sure that I'd never appear in another movie. I'd also worry about my acting. Let's face it—nobody ever gets to the point where he can truly say, 'I now know it all!' "

*CHAPTER VII*

# MR. SMITH GOES TO WAR

"Jimmy seldom talks about his war experiences," said Bill Grady, who had become MGM's chief casting director. "When you ask him, he turns red or else turns pale and clams up. It's been that way from the very beginning. He tried to make his military service a very private thing. Of course, it was all but impossible. I was asked to take him to his physical. The studio assigned us a long, black limousine, but he didn't want anything so ostentatious. Instead, he went by trolley. I finally tailed him to the Army medical center, where I was told that Jimmy had made it by a single ounce. 'That fellow sure is an oddball,' a sergeant told me. 'Didn't even complain when he found out that he'd been accepted.'

"What the sergeant didn't know was that Jimmy was so determined to pass the weight test that he hadn't allowed himself a bowel or bladder movement in thirty-six hours. It must have been torture, but it did put him over."

MGM tried to convince Stewart's draft board that he was needed on the home front. "Jimmy refused to cooperate," said Louis B. Mayer, the studio head. "I couldn't understand him. Although I'm probably more public spirited than the next man, you've got to remember that this was nine months before Pearl Harbor. That bullhead really wanted to go into the service and no amount of talking helped. There was nothing to do but give in."

"Mayer wanted to fly the MGM flag at half mast," Grady said. "He arranged for a huge going-away party. Actors gave sentimental, patriotic, impassioned toasts. Actresses couldn't stop kissing Jimmy. Some wept. Rosalind Russell took out her handkerchief to wipe lipstick off his face. Underneath each red stain, she printed the name of the star who did the kissing. Jimmy kept it for a good luck omen. The tears as he left were not from onions. They were real."

The next night, Grady gave Stewart another farewell party. He had borrowed actor Franchot Tone's lavish home for the occasion. On each tree that lined the path to the house hung an elegant Japanese lantern. "It looked like an Oriental fairyland," Jimmy recalled. "I was early, and only Bill and several other people were there. Suddenly, Bill said to one of the female guests who was wearing a long black evening gown, 'Miss Smith, you're wanted on the phone.' Bill's parties were always offbeat, and I should have expected something. When she turned to walk to the house, I could see that she didn't have any back to the dress— it had been carefully cut out. That kind of set the tone for the rest of the evening."

However, it all changed radically the following morning. With the other inductees, Stewart lined up and vowed: "I, James Maitland Stewart, do solemnly swear that I will bear true faith and allegiance to the United States of America and will serve it honestly and faithfully against all its enemies whomsoever. I will obey orders of the President of the United States and the officers appointed over me according to the rules of the articles of war. So help me, God."

"You could tell he meant every single word," said Francis Mullens. "I was standing next to him when the oath was administered. We had both been drafted at the same time and took our basic training together. Dozens of his fans would wait outside

JHAN ROBBINS

the wire gate to catch a glimpse of him as he walked by. Even
in the rain. Reporters and newsreel cameras singled him out.

"At the beginning he would get several dozen phone calls a
day. Most of them were from admirers—young female admirers.
I understand several made some pretty bawdy and outright proposals. Things got to be so confusing and embarrassing that
Jimmy started refusing overnight passes. What's more, the scut-
tlebutt was that he had turned down a thousand dollars a week
his studio wanted to send him regularly. He settled to get along
like his buddies on a lousy $21 a month. Who does that vol-
untarily? We felt the poor bastard should be given a section
eight. [A mental discharge.] I don't mind telling you we were
damn jealous. But after a couple of weeks, we realized Jimmy
was really okay."

Stewart was particularly delighted with a private named Simpson. "We had both landed at Moffett Field at the same time,"
he said. "A short while later, we were sent down to be issued
uniforms. When it came Simpson's turn to be given shoes, the
supply corporal asked him what size he wore. The corporal thought
he was getting some smart-alecky answer when he was told, 'Size
fifteen, four A.'

" 'Okay, wise guy,' the corporal snapped, 'what's your real
size?'

" 'Fifteen, four A,' Simpson repeated as he pointed to his feet.
I've never seen such a turmoil when it became obvious that he
hadn't been lying. One look at those feet and immediately you
knew he was telling the truth. The corporal called a sergeant,
who called a lieutenant. The three of them kept staring and
shaking their heads. I surely thought that Simpson would be
discharged. But a couple of weeks later, he proudly showed me
a pair of new GI shoes that had been made especially for him."

Ten months later, Stewart was commissioned a second lieutenant and received his pilot wings. "Before going into the Army
Air Corps," Jimmy said, "I had hundreds of private flying hours,
but I don't think there ever was a prouder pilot than I was when
those wings were pinned on me."

53

He expected to be sent overseas. Instead he was given a radio publicity job. "My instructions were to make soldiers laugh," he recalled. "For three months I traded so many jokes with Edgar Bergen and Charlie McCarthy that I was beginning to feel that I, too, had been carved out of wood."

Just as he was beginning to think that the assignment would last for the duration, he was transferred to flight instructor's school. Then he was made a member of the faculty. His rank was now first lieutenant. "It was a cushy post," said retired Major Samuel Brantley. "Stewart could have been doing that until the war ended, but he kept asking for European or Pacific assignments. After much pestering, he got his wish."

In November of 1943, Jimmy was ordered overseas. Before departing, he had a final reunion with his father. When he was ready to leave, Alex handed him an envelope. "Don't read it until you're in transit," he whispered.

Frank Hood, associate editor of the *Indiana Evening Gazette*, said, "Alex was never one to act restrained and mask his true feelings, but this time he managed to. Jimmy said that the envelope contained a note and a copy of the ninety-first Psalm:

> I will say of the Lord, He is my refuge and my fortress . . .
> His truth shall be thy shield and buckler.
> Thou shalt not be afraid for the terror by night, nor for the
> arrow that flieth by day . . .
> For He shall give his angels charge over thee, to keep thee in all
> thy ways. They shall bear thee up in their hands, lest thou
> dash thy foot against a stone . . .

He choked up when he remembered his father's closing sentences: "Goodby, my dear son. God bless you and keep you. I love you far more than I can possibly tell you. Dad."

Eleven days after arriving in England, Stewart led the 703rd Bomber Squadron on an air strike against Kiel, Germany's main naval base. This was quickly followed by other missions. After a particularly violent attack on Ludwigshafen, another important target, he was praised for his "leadership ability and good judgment." The crisp commendation did not reveal the grim story of savage Luftwaffe resistance that caused heavy losses among American planes. But Jimmy always brought his squadron back intact.

Steve Kirkpatrick had been a navigator attached to the 703rd. "Stewart was a damn good commanding officer," he said. "Even if he went rigidly by the book. But I always had the feeling that he would never ask you to do something he wouldn't do himself. Everything that man did seemed to go like clockwork. However, there was one incident that sure kicked up a lot of fuss. Jimmy had supposedly communicated directly with the British royal family without going through proper military channels.

"Later I learned what actually occurred was that one of his movie fans had requested the Queen Mother to forward a message to him. Somehow the entire U.S. Army and the R.A.F. got involved. Before it was straightened out, all hell broke loose."

Jimmy had been away from the floodlights and cameras so long that he got flustered at a news briefing he was asked to conduct. An entire newsreel had to be done over. Stewart apologized. "In Hollywood, they let you do things over," he told the assembled reporters, "but out here the first take is what counts. I promise it won't happen again."

It didn't. Ernie Pyle, the famous war correspondent, called Jimmy's subsequent briefings brisk and informative. Bernard Lerner, who was a captain in the aerial photography division, said, "Stewart supplied us with some of the best pictures we had. And you could always count on his reports."

After an extremely hazardous raid over Brunswick, Germany, Jimmy was awarded the Distinguished Flying Cross by General Jimmy Doolittle. The citation reads:

> In spite of aggressive fighter attacks and later heavy accurate anti-aircraft fire, Major James Maitland Stewart was able to hold the formation together and direct a successful bombing run over the target. The courage, leadership and skillful bombing airmanship

displayed by him were in a large measure responsible for the success of this mission.

When Jimmy found time, he would send his friends brief notes urging them to aid the war effort. Bill Grady recalled one he received when the fighting in Europe had ended. "This part may be over," Stewart had written, "but don't let up. We still have a lot of work to do."

Somehow, agent-producer Leland Hayward had learned that Jimmy was returning home aboard the *Queen Elizabeth*, which had been turned into a giant troop carrier. Hayward managed to meet the ship as tugs guided it into New York's West 15th Street pier. "Let's go," he said as he spotted the lanky officer, now a full colonel. "Your mother and father are waiting for you at the St. Regis Hotel."

Stewart, then thirty-seven years old, still had a baby face, although his hair was a little grayer. "Wait a few minutes," he replied. "I want to stay until a few of my boys come ashore."

"The wait grew longer and longer," Hayward said. " 'Those boys must be off by now!' I told him. 'By the way, how many are there?' When Jimmy told me, 'I guess a couple of hundred,' he wasn't being cute. I should have known he'd do something like that. One of them, a technical sergeant, saluted him. Jimmy saluted back. Then he said to me, 'There goes a real courageous man!'

"I replied something maudlin but oh so true: 'That makes two!' "

# CHAPTER VIII

# DOES JIMMY STILL HAVE IT?

Studio executives wanted to give Stewart a lavish ticker-tape parade when he returned from the war. "He's a hero," said George Stevens, a Hollywood director. "He's got medals to prove it." (Jimmy was awarded the Distinguished Flying Cross with Oak Leaf Cluster, the Air Medal, the *Croix de Guerre* and seven battle stars.)

Jimmy refused, saying, "Thousands of men in uniform did far more meaningful things and got small recognition, if any."

Stevens wasn't too surprised at the reluctance: "Someone else saying that would have made me skeptical. But coming from him, it was an entirely different story."

Back home, many townspeople urged him to run for governor of Pennsylvania. They pointed out how effective he'd been in *Mr. Smith Goes to Washington*. Jimmy listened patiently. "That's not such a good idea," he said. "It's only in pictures that I make a good office holder. And what's even more important—I talk much too slowly for a politician!"

It was also suggested that he become a director. While he had been away, many stars had set up their own moviemaking companies with themselves as majority stockholders. He was told that it was the smart thing to do. "I think it's foolish," he replied. "I spent years learning to act. Why try something else?"

Although Stewart was warmly welcomed back, Hollywood producers had doubts about his four-year absence from film-making. Could he still stand the pace? Was his personality outdated? Was he still a name? And how well would the public receive his current movies?

His contract with MGM had expired during the period he had served in the Air Force. He cast his lot with Liberty Films, an independent studio that had recently been formed by Stevens, Frank Capra and William Wyler.

"They are savvy and honorable people," he said. He insisted, however, that an "anti-hero" clause be inserted in the agreement: "In all advertising and publicity issued by the corporation, or under its control, the corporation will not mention or cause to be mentioned the part taken by the artist in World War II as an officer of the U.S. Army."

"The film he made for us was *It's a Wonderful Life*," said Frank Capra, the picture's director. "On the very first day of shooting, he arrived on the set at 5:00 A.M. He was not supposed to be there until an hour later. 'I just wanted to be sure I was on time,' he drawled. It was that way until the final scene. He was easily the most prompt and obliging person on the lot."

Donna Reed, Stewart's co-star, recalled his diligence: "Several days before we had to report for work, Jimmy asked Frank Capra what scene he planned on shooting first. Jimmy told me that he studied that scene forward and backward until he could recite it in his sleep. Imagine his horror when Frank apologized for giving him the wrong starting scene. Instead of the one he had rehearsed, we did one where I ask him if he'll walk me home.

"In the scene, Jimmy swallowed so hard I could hear the sound even though I was several feet away. He stuttered slower than usual. 'N . . . O!' he finally squawked.

"Frank was delighted. 'Jimmy,' he shouted, 'that was just right! You haven't lost your touch!'

"Jimmy grinned and reached for my hand. He squeezed it. I

could tell he was very relieved. From that moment on, most things went smoothly."

Mollie Sugarman, the studio's girl Friday, disagreed. "Let me tell you there were plenty of headaches making that movie," she said. "Some days it seemed that nothing would go right. For instance, when the scene called for Jimmy to be sitting at a bar looking exhausted and dejected. He appeared to be so unhappy that one of the extras kept patting him on the back. We had to do that scene over and over, until Joe Biroc, one of the cameramen, ran out of film.

"If that wasn't bad enough, Thomas Mitchell, who was also in the movie, broke his glasses—frame and all. I was given the job of getting him another pair. I managed to, but they were the wrong color frames; Mr. Capra felt they were a shade too dark. The next pair wasn't right either. On my third try, Mr. Capra grudgingly allowed Mitchell to wear them.

"At the end of that day's shooting, I passed Jimmy in the hall. I must have looked so haggard that he said, 'Sometimes I think we chose the wrong business, Mollie. Maybe I should have stuck to architecture.' Then he asked me about my previous work. When I told him that I had helped make spark plugs in a war factory, he seemed delighted. 'It's people like you that won the war!' he said.

"That night I went home singing." She then added, "Audiences expected Jimmy Stewart to make clean pictures—and he always obliged. Why, in that movie it took more than a thousand feet of film before he got around to kissing the heroine. Yet, some of the sexiest actresses wanted him for their leading man. He's unlike the other actors I've ever worked with—a moral, high-minded gentleman. Even more so when he came back from the war."

"World War II had a tremendous effect on me," said Stewart. "It really turned my thinking around. But it's quite untrue, as some stories have stated, that I was so disillusioned that I wanted to leave the acting business. Some people claimed that when I took my uniform off, I wondered if moviemaking was right for a grown man. That's plain nonsense.

"I've never had any doubts about being an actor. However, my feelings were strengthened by something Lionel Barrymore told me while we were making *It's a Wonderful Life*. I was terribly influenced by what he said: 'Jimmy, don't ever forget that acting is the greatest profession ever invented. When you act you move millions of people, shape their lives, give them a sense of exaltation. No other profession has that power.' "

Stewart's performance in *It's a Wonderful Life* was enthusiastically applauded by most critics. *New York Times:* "As the hero of this film, Mr. Stewart does a warmly appealing job, indicating that he has grown in spiritual stature as well as in talent during the years he was in the war." *Newsweek:* "Stewart's adult, appealing, postwar impersonation of the frustrated stay-at-home who learns that wealth is measured in terms of people he can call friends is one of the year's ranking performances."

Dissenting critics for Boston and San Francisco newspapers called the movie "corny" and "banal." Jimmy rarely contradicted reviewers, but this time he felt he had to speak out. "I don't understand," he said. "True, we recently haven't been doing too well in kindness and humility. But still, both qualities are so essential for happiness in real life."

In spite of the scoffers, Stewart received his third Academy Award nomination. When he failed to win the Oscar, Lionel Barrymore exclaimed, "That was a confounded mistake! I don't want to belittle Freddy March's performance in *Best Years of Our Lives*, but Jimmy was better!"

Liberty Films folded, and Stewart decided to freelance. The following year, he made *Call Northside 777* for 20th Century-Fox. He played a crusading reporter—the ninth time he had been cast as a newspaperman. He did it so convincingly that the National Press Club advised future movie reporters to study him closely. They issued a list of five Jimmy Stewart *doesn'ts:*

1. Jimmy doesn't sit on the publisher's desk and tell him how to run his paper.
2. Jimmy doesn't remove a whiskey bottle from his rear pocket and swig it between cigarette puffs.

3. Jimmy doesn't always wear a press card in the band of his hat.
4. Jimmy doesn't dress like a tramp, hang out in bars and leer at all pretty women.
5. Jimmy doesn't roll up his wet raincoat in a ball, throw it at a fellow reporter and slam the typewriter carriage back and forth before starting the story. In short, Jimmy Stewart always plays an authentic newspaperman who loves his wife and children, worries about a mortgage and dreams about a raise.

Jimmy has always found it necessary to study carefully the character he's playing. "However, I'm not what you'd call a method actor," he said. "I've always been skeptical of people who say they lose themselves in a part. Someone once asked Spencer Tracy if he was tired of always playing Tracy. He replied, 'What am I supposed to do, play Bogart?' "

Yet, Stewart's characterization of a one-legged baseball pitcher—a part Ronald Reagan wanted to play—was so unerring that Monty Stratton, the man he was portraying, said, "When I saw Jimmy on the screen, I wept. He was more me than I am!"

It went like this: MGM had asked Stewart to star in *The Stratton Story*. It was a true account of a promising young Chicago White Sox pitcher whose leg had to be amputated because of a hunting accident. After several poignant years, Monty Stratton returned to the baseball diamond equipped with an artificial leg.

For three months, Jimmy studied the crippled pitcher. Five hours a day were spent with major league ballplayers who gave him batting and pitching instruction. He talked to orthopedic surgeons and physical therapy specialists. To achieve the effect of having a false leg, Stewart wore a steel harness all day that forced him to limp.

Again, reviewers were stirred. *New York Times:* "Mr. Stewart gives such a winning performance that it's almost impossible to imagine anyone else playing the role." *Baseball News:* "Not only does Jimmy Stewart imitate Monty Stratton perfectly, but he looks like he really belongs in the big league. He's a major leaguer through and through."

In the late forties, Jimmy's handprints were added to the cement at the entrance to Hollywood's Grauman's Chinese Theater. Archie Henderson, a popcorn salesclerk in the theater's outdoor snack stand, recently said, "People from all over the world come to gawk. Only yesterday, a middle-aged woman from London curtsied to them. But that was mild compared to what a lady did a couple of months ago. She was so moved when she saw his handprints that she kept coming back every afternoon with a bucket filed with soap and water. She scrubbed like mad. 'I want Jimmy to always be clean,' she kept explaining."

## CHAPTER IX

# THE MOST ELIGIBLE BACHELOR IN BEVERLY HILLS

Although neither romantic nor swashbuckling, Stewart dated some of the screen's loveliest, most exciting women—a spectrum of personalities ranging from screen empresses to artistic intellectuals: Margaret Sullavan, Jean Harlow, Ginger Rogers, Olivia de Havilland, Alice Faye, Lana Turner, Norma Shearer, Dorothy Lamour, Marlene Dietrich.

"The more exotic the woman, the more deceptively simple Jimmy became," said producer Joseph Pasternak. "When Marlene got on the set of *Destry Rides Again*, she took one look at him and said, 'That's for me!' He didn't seem to be aware of what she had in mind. He was in love—with Flash Gordon, the comic book character. That's all he seemed to read, all that occupied his attention. Marlene decided to take the initiative. She had the art department make a life-sized doll of Flash Gordon that was correct in every way. Then she walked into his dressing room, handed over the gift and locked the three of them in together."

"Who will be Mrs. Jimmy Stewart?" became a favorite Hollywood guessing game. From 1935 to 1949, more than a hundred stories discussing Stewart's marital status appeared in movie fan magazines. Many with intriguing titles:

WHAT DOES JIMMY STEWART THINK OF WOMEN?

"I WANT THE GIRL NEXT DOOR," SAYS HOLLYWOOD'S
MOST ELIGIBLE BACHELOR

JIMMY'S AFRAID OF A SCREEN-STYLE MARRIAGE!

Repeatedly, Stewart was interviewed about his plans for matrimony. He had a stock answer: "Most of the actresses I date are fine women, but I'm still looking."

In his early Hollywood days, he and Cary Grant, another reluctant-to-marry, gave a wild bachelor party that the film capital still remembers. Barbara Carroll, then a starlet who had been told that she was a second Joan Crawford, described the affair: "I've been to some scale-ten parties, but this was scale-eleven! I don't know how I rated an invitation, so I asked. 'Because you're 34-22-34,' I was told. Blunt, see!

"All the stops were pulled out. Mike Romanoff did the catering. There were gardenias all over the place—it smelled like the Forest Lawn cemetery. Pink champagne was actually poured into the ladies' slippers. I remember Jimmy saying, 'Thank God, there aren't too many open-toed shoes.'

"One of the guests got roaring drunk and started making passes at the women—I was one of them. Jimmy saw what was happening and quickly put a stop to it. I don't know what he said, but it sure worked. I watched him as he walked the man to the door and practically tossed him out.

"I was very grateful and tried to thank him, but was drowned out by the music. Bing Crosby had taken over the piano—and he sure wasn't quiet. He went through his entire bag of songs. We all joined Jimmy and Cary in singing 'Auld Lang Syne' when the party ended—at 9 A.M.!"

The gala received a great deal of publicity. A few days after it occurred, a young woman rang Stewart's doorbell. The maid answered. "I'm Jimmy's cousin," the visitor said. "Only he has never met me."

She was told to wait in the living room. As soon as the actor

When Jimmy was three (1911), he rode a nice shiny tricycle which his dad, Alex Stewart, took out of his Indiana, Pennsylvania, hardware store stock and presented to the boy.

Jimmy, his parents and two sisters just before his father went overseas in World War I. Young Stewart made his mother buy him a boy's army uniform he refused to take off. (Courtesy *The Indiana* [Pa.] *Gazette*)

Stewart at the start of his movie career. "I've never been a Hollywood glamour boy," he said. "I'm no Arrow collar ad." (AP/Wide World Photos)

He played a minor role in MGM's *After the Thin Man.* Myrna Loy, who starred with him in the film, said, "You could tell that very soon he'd be given leading parts."

Jimmy was miscast opposite French movie star Simone Simon in a remake of *Seventh Heaven.* He played a Paris sewer worker who falls in love with a street waif.

In *It's a Wonderful World,* Jimmy was a self-acclaimed master private eye who joins forces with Claudette Colbert, a scatterbrained poetess.

Critics hailed Stewart's performance as the naive and idealistic U.S. senator in *Mr. Smith Goes to Washington.*

Katharine Hepburn, who starred with Cary Grant and Stewart in *The Philadelphia Story,* called Jimmy "a real professional—he knows how to steal a movie."

In 1941 Jimmy won an Oscar for his performance in *The Philadelphia Story*. His onetime girlfriend, Ginger Rogers, received one for her performance in *Kitty Foyle*. (AP/Wide World Photos)

Nine months before Pearl Harbor, Stewart joined the armed forces.
MGM wanted him deferred, but he refused and came home a
colonel and wing commander of the Eighth Air Force.

Lieutenant James Maitland Stewart visited his family in Indiana,
Pennsylvania, as often as possible. (Courtesy *The Indiana* [Pa.] *Gazette*)

Jimmy starred in *The Stratton Story,* the true account of a baseball pitcher who, after losing a leg in a hunting accident, returned to the big leagues with the help of his wife (June Allyson). "When I saw Jimmy on the screen, I wept," said the real Stratton. "He was more me than I am!"

At the age of forty-one, Jimmy finally took a bride, beautiful social-ite Gloria Hatrick McLean.
(AP/ Wide World Photos)

One of Stewart's outstanding successes was his performance in *Harvey*, as the invisible six-foot rabbit's whimsical, pixilated companion, Elwood P. Dowd.

In Cecil B. De Mille's circus epic, *The Greatest Show on Earth*, the audience never saw Jimmy's face without his clown makeup. "Few other big name actors would completely hide their identity," said actress Gloria Grahame.

"I guess I'm just double-lucky," said Jimmy when he became the proud father of Judith and Kelly. Wife Gloria agreed.

appeared, she began to disrobe and to make suggestive remarks. Jimmy was terrified but quickly realized it was part of a not very subtle plot. "Cousin, my foot!" he yelled. "Better get out of here before I call the cops!" No sooner had she fled, when the bell sounded again. This time the caller was the long-lost cousin's husband, pretending to be outraged. But he had arrived too late; Jimmy had successfully thwarted the blackmail scheme.

"Girls were always after him," said Bill Grady, MGM's casting director. "I once asked him how one of his romances was working out. It was with a pretty redheaded starlet. He got a puzzled look on his face. 'I'm not so sure,' he told me. 'I just don't understand her.' Later I found out they had been parked outside of her house on a moonlit night. The dame felt romantic and said, 'It's so lovely; the trolls must be out tonight.' If she'd said elves or pixies or leprechauns, Jimmy might have gotten it, but trolls didn't register with him so he asked, 'Who are the Trolls—your neighbors?' The dame stared a him, ran inside and slammed the door."

A few days later, the starlet telephoned to say that all was forgiven. To show that she bore no ill will, she invited him over for dinner; he accepted. When he arrived, he donned an apron and offered to help. That's when he noticed a shiny, streamlined electric beater in her kitchen. Well-known for being gadget-happy, he inquired about it. He was enthralled when he learned that it could be adapted to a number of culinary uses.

That night, he and his hostess sat up until two A.M., grinding meat, crushing ice and grating onions. He still speaks of that night "as a most delightful experience." Needless to say, it was the very last time the young lady invited him over!

One of Stewart's first serious romances was with actress Norma Shearer, widow of Irving Thalberg, MGM's head producer. Jimmy sat next to her at a formal studio party. After his third glass of wine, he told her that she was the most enchanting creature he had ever seen.

"From that moment on she staked her claim," said Josh Logan. "She'd drive him all over town in her long, yellow limousine. Whenever the limo passed someone he knew, he slumped to the floor so as not to be recognized."

65

George Stevens asked Jimmy about the strange behavior. "One moment you're sitting in full view," the director said. "Then you disappear. What gives?"

The embarrassed actor stuttered more than usual. In an almost inaudible whisper, he told Stevens, "The car seat gets mighty uncomfortable . . . I find it better for my back when I . . . sit on the floor."

"Norma was quite possessive," said Logan. "She wanted people to understand that Jimmy was hers. She gave him a solid gold cigarette case studded with dozens of diamonds. I'm sure she did it on purpose—so that when she asked for a cigarette in front of other people, her expensive gift would advertise the fact that she was the giver. But Jimmy, not wanting to see sly looks, would fumble in all his pockets until he found a crumpled pack of Lucky Strikes. They were his badge as a free man."

Some of the macho-looking male stars were unhappy about competition from the underweight beanpole. They tried to spread rumors that the actresses really weren't romantically interested in him, but that he aroused their motherly instincts. However, marriage proposals arrived regularly—most of them not very motherly. A nineteen-year-old Dallas secretary wrote: "I don't want to brag, but my friends tell me that I'm beautiful, talented and would make some man a superb wife!"

A twenty-four-year-old Cleveland teacher: "Your way of talking and grinning gives me goose bumps."

A seventeen-year-old student in a San Francisco beauty culture school: "The stars reveal that I'm to walk by your side."

Politely, Stewart thanked the writers but said that he was much too busy making movies to oblige them. "I don't have time to fool around," he told a reporter. "Often, I have to work on Sundays. Now, I ask you, how can ardent love thrive under such conditions?"

Despite the heavy work schedule, Jimmy continued to be the fan magazines' number-one bachelor. Every month they had him engaged—often to the leading lady of his current picture. Two of his dates drew more attention than the others: Ginger Rogers and Olivia de Havilland.

One overzealous writer spotted Jimmy and Ginger having lunch in a secluded seaside restaurant. She watched the couple gaze at a white sheet of paper, then heatedly discuss it. Immediately, she called her editor. "Jimmy finally did it!" she shrieked into the receiver. "I just saw the marriage license!"

The white sheet of paper turned out to be a horoscope the San Francisco beauty student had sent Stewart. The incorrect details didn't faze the editor; his next story was even more fanciful. It claimed that the couple were tired of Hollywood and planned to start a sheep ranch in Australia right after their wedding.

The gossip columnists and fan magazine writers wore out their typewriters when Jimmy was squiring Olivia de Havilland. Walter Winchell, the widely syndicated columnist, said, "Their first date got more coverage than did Orson Welles' famous *War of the Worlds* radio scare!"

De Havilland recalled the initial meeting. "I had played Melanie in *Gone With the Wind*," she said. "At the New York premiere Irene Selznick arranged for Jimmy to be my escort. At the time I didn't know him, just about him. To me he was one more American hero, much like Charles Lindbergh had been. Jimmy met me at the airport in a rented limousine. I remember how impressed I was because he managed to have the auto driven right up to my plane. We didn't say much that night, but I could tell that he liked me. I certainly liked him. We started seeing one another regularly."

A few weeks later, he called for her in a convertible LaSalle that he had just bought. "It was very slick and shiny," Stewart recalled. "I was sure she'd be impressed. I made sure the hand brake was on, because Olivia lived on the top of a steep hill. Then I went inside to get her. As we came out, the LaSalle started moving by itself."

Jimmy ran after it, but it picked up speed as it continued its descent. Along the way it grazed other cars, tore up shrubbery, knocked down fences and finally was stopped by a telephone pole. "Most expensive car I ever owned," Stewart moaned.

Olivia, however, was amused. "I believe I told him that he certainly knew how to entertain his date," she said. "That's one of the few times he didn't grin. But he usually was such good company to be with—a grownup Huck Finn."

They broke up when friends began to tell one another that marriage was imminent. "Jimmy wasn't ready for a wife," Olivia said. "I guess he still had to sow wild oats."

Stewart explained the breakup of the romance with humor. "I had to stop going out with Olivia de Havilland," he mused, "because I never could say her name properly when I had to introduce her."

Leland Hayward, Stewart's friend and agent, was always trying to find him a wife. "The movie business is fickle," he'd say. "Get yourself a rich girl and settle down."

One afternoon when Jimmy was in Hayward's office, the agent said, "I've just met the right woman for you. She's rolling in dough. Besides she's not too bad looking. Why don't you take her to dinner?"

Jimmy did. As soon as he returned home, Leland telephoned. When he learned that nothing had happened, he was indignant. "Did you remember to bring her flowers?" he asked. Again, the reply was negative. "Don't you realize that all females love posies?" he bellowed.

Several days later, a very surprised Stewart received a thank-you note from the girl: "Your lovely roses filled the entire house. It was sweet of you to send them to me before I move to Paris." Jimmy never saw her again, but he did see the florist's bill for $515. Hayward had ordered ten dozen long-stemmed roses and charged them to Stewart.

Another person who frequently nagged him about taking a wife was his father. Repeatedly, Alex quoted the Bible to his bachelor son: "It is not good for man to live alone . . ."

"I'm still looking," Jimmy would reply earnestly.

# CHAPTER X

# THE GREAT AMERICAN BACHELOR
# TAKES A BRIDE

At the age of forty-one, Jimmy finally took a bride. "By that time a lot of big Hollywood stars are working on their third or fourth wife," said Lew Wasserman, the head of MCA-Universal. "But that's not for him. He's very old fashioned about such an important step. Why, even in a movie, he didn't pop the question until the last reel!"

Reaction of the fan magazines was predictable—they were devastated. "Now that the G.A.B. (Great American Bachelor) is about to say, 'I do,' " ran one story, "there's no longer hope for any of us. So we girls might as well slit our throats."

Stewart's bride-to-be was Gloria Hatrick McLean, former wife of millionaire Edward McLean, Jr. (His mother, Evelyn Walsh McLean, owned the famous Hope Diamond.) Gloria had never acted in films and had no desire to start. She did, however, know a great deal about the entertainment world. Her father was head of MGM's legal staff. Ten years younger than Stewart, she was a very pretty woman who had two young sons from her previous marriage. *Vogue* magazine described her as being "Refreshingly handsome, with large green eyes, clearly marked brows and loosely-combed, bright brown hair. She looks in casual clothes the way most people hope they will look in casual clothes."

Gloria was regularly summoned to high society functions but turned most of them down. "I prefer the outdoors by day and quiet evenings at home," she explained. She did, however, accept an invitation from the Gary Coopers to attend one of their elaborate dinner parties. Stewart, the extra man, was seated next to her. Their conversation was brief, but she managed to tell him that she had two boys, four and five years old, liked golf and was very interested in conservation.

"I could tell right off that she was a thoroughbred," said Jimmy, who escorted her home from the Coopers' dinner party. "Gloria maintains that it wasn't our first meeting; that we had met each other many months before. I can't honestly recall that historic occasion. Probably because at the time my head was buzzing from too much eggnog. It was the custom at Christmas to get together with my pals and visit a lot of our friends' homes. Naturally, we'd be invited in. Gloria tells me that she was sitting on the doorstep at Keenan Wynn's house, getting a breath of fresh air, when three of us stumbled up the steps. She says that we were the sorriest-looking trio she'd ever seen."

"The romance very nearly broke up before it got started," Gloria recalled. "At the time, I had a beautiful big German police dog named Bellow. When Jimmy saw me to the door, Bellow took one look at the strange man and went for his jugular."

Stewart returned the following afternoon for a golf date. "For me," said Jimmy, "it had been love at first sight. She was the kind of a girl I had always dreamed of. The kind you associate with open country, cooking stew and not fainting because it was made of cut-up squirrels. She'd look at home on a sailboat or a raft; in a graceful spring from a tree branch into the swimming hole or from a high diving board into a country club swimming pool. But I realized that I first had to woo the dog. I bought him steaks at Chasen's. I prattled baby talk to him. Patted him. Praised him. It got to be pretty humiliating, but we finally got to be friends. I was free to court Gloria. We continued to see one another. And after almost a year of going steady, we became engaged."

At the time, he was filming a Western called *Broken Arrow*. It was one of the first movies to present the American Indian in a sympathetic light—not as a mindless savage. Historian Will Durant said, "The movie contributed a great deal to soften the hearts of racists. Probably more than thousands of speeches and books. Stewart is to be commended."

Jimmy was cast as a frontier scout who studies Indian culture, learns to speak their language and marries an Apache maiden. He acts as mediator between the tribe and hostile whites. Jeff Chandler, who played Cochise, chief of the Chiricahua Apaches, said, "I know it was only a movie role, but Jimmy did it so convincingly, he made everyone realize that Indians are also members of the human race."

Gloria came to watch the filming. The script called for a love scene between Stewart and the Indian girl he marries, a role played by Debra Paget. Director Delmer Daves noticed Jimmy's nervousness. "I'm sure," he reassured his male star, "that your fiancée has no objections if you make love to your leading lady."

Stewart turned his gaze upon his betrothed, as if waiting for a formal approval. She had overheard Daves's comment. "Absolutely none," she replied. "And he better make a good job of it, too. He's going to be the breadwinner in the family. And if he has to make love to women, I want him to do it better than anyone else. That is cinematically speaking, of course!"

Although Stewart's marriage plans were widely circulated, a publicist for 20th Century-Fox announced that Jimmy was still a bachelor in the eyes of the Indians. He instructed Jess Thunder Cloud, an important member of the tribe, to express regret that the forty-one-year-old actor "still walked the trouble-path of life without the comforting help of a squaw."

Thunder Cloud, feeling sorry for Stewart, offered him the hand of his daughter, Teesa, fifteen. "She will make you a fine wife because she is well trained in weaving and cooking," he said. "All I ask in return are three horses and a milk cow."

The promotional stunt had started off harmlessly but got out of hand. Many of the other Indians took it seriously and contributed to Teesa's dowry: turquoise necklaces, blankets, doeskin blouses, handwoven baskets and papoose carriers. Jimmy managed to appease them by saying that Thunder Cloud's daughter was indeed lovely and talented, but he didn't have any horses or a milk cow.

Jimmy and Gloria were married on August 9, 1949, in the chapel of the Brentwood Presbyterian Church. Eighteen guests were present. Among them, Mr. and Mrs. Alexander Stewart (Gloria's parents were too ill to attend), the Gary Coopers, the David Nivens, Spencer Tracy and Mike Romanoff. Outside, more than 500 admirers waited for the couple to leave the church. They were reserved, unlike most Hollywood mobs. Jimmy had said he hoped there wouldn't be any disturbance. That morning, a columnist reported that Stewart was infuriated when a newspaper photographer asked if he might take pictures of the bride dressing for the nuptials.

"No!" snapped Jimmy.

"But I do it for all the screen weddings," the photographer replied. "It's customary."

"At this wedding, it is not!" Jimmy bellowed.

The crowd was silent throughout the twelve-minute ceremony. When the couple emerged there was no press for souvenirs. They gawked at the bride and bridegroom but made no attempt to stop them. Policemen stationed to maintain order had little to do. "Jimmy seems to bring out the best in us," one of them said.

A guest at the wedding said, "The only hullabaloo was made by Jimmy's father—the wedding took place in a part of the church that wasn't finished yet. The guests had to sit on chairs instead of pews. So what does old man Stewart do? He goes around to everybody and asks them to give money to buy pews!"

The honeymoon was postponed so that Jimmy could serve as Grand Marshal of the National Soap Box Derby. "I had given my word I'd be there," he said. "Gloria understands the importance of a promise." A few days later, they flew to Hawaii. Their holiday was cut short when they returned to the mainland for the funeral of Gloria's father.

The newly married couple and Gloria's two young sons moved into a thirty-two-year-old Tudor-style eight-room house in Beverly Hills. (A simple place, it suits their tastes; they still live there.) At the time, Jimmy had started a new movie. He wasn't fully aware that husbands are required to kiss wives goodby before leaving for work. Suddenly, he'd remember that he was married—slam on the brakes and head for the nearest telephone booth. When his new wife answered, he'd say meekly, "Goodby, dear." Then he'd buss the receiver.

In less than two years, Jimmy Stewart was the proud father of four children: Ronald and Michael, stepsons, and Judith and Kelly, twin daughters of his own. The two girls were born on May 7, 1951. Although they were pronounced in good health, doctors feared for the infants' mother. For ten days, Gloria's life was in jeopardy. The hospital was deluged with get-well letters, telegrams and phone calls. Religious medals and bottles of holy water arrived by special delivery.

"I've never seen such an outpouring of love and concern," said Elizabeth Goodman, a nurse who helped care for Mrs. Stewart. "Her husband was there around the clock. He wouldn't leave her bedside. We pleaded with him to go home and get some sleep, but he ignored us and just sat. Sometimes, I'd see him praying. He didn't eat. The doctors feared for his health, too. I'd bring him a sandwich or some fruit. In the morning, I'd find them uneaten.

"When Mrs. Stewart was ready to be discharged, he was so excited that he nearly drove his car into the lobby. We got his wife ready, then he took off in a mad dash. But he forgot one important thing—Mrs. Stewart. He had forgotten to put her in the car. A short time later he came back, apologizing."

Jimmy liked being a family man. "There's never any loneliness now, not with Gloria and the kids around," he said. "As a bachelor, I used to get up late on Sundays, play golf, have dates. Now it's our most important day of the week. We all have breakfast together. Then we go to church, where Gloria teaches Sunday School. The rest of the day we picnic or hike or just stay at home together.

"When I'm not on camera, all of us spend a lot of time together. However, we don't overdo it—kids need some privacy. I've also

73

found out that they welcome discipline. A good smack in the right place is still the most effective way to point the way. But you have to remember to treat each child according to his or her personality. We don't have a specific formula—just sound common sense and a feeling of give and take. It's the kind of upbringing I had when I was growing up."

Gloria agrees. "But I'm afraid I sometimes turned to Jimmy for discipline," she said. "Like the time young Ronnie tossed a ball at one of my best lamps. He smashed it to pieces. I knew that if I punished him, it wouldn't mean a thing, but if he saw Jimmy was actually angry enough to spank him, it would register."

"So, I rolled up my sleeves," Stewart recalled, "and went to work in the same way my dad used to remind me that I needed to remember my transgressions."

Shortly after they were married, Jimmy had to go to England to film *No Highway in the Sky* for 20th Century-Fox. He was told that he'd be away for at least five months. "That was entirely too long a separation," he said. "Gloria and I decided that the four of us should go—the girls weren't born yet. It turned out to be a wonderful experience for the two boys. The high point was a command performance we attended. Ronnie was asked to present a bouquet to the queen. He did it just right, even if he ran away right after he handed Her Royal Highness the flowers. Kids are a lot more resilient than we think—they can often handle situations that we adults find ticklish."

Jimmy is very enthusiastic about being the father of twins. "Everybody should have at least one set," he said happily. "They play with each other. It just isn't true they're double-trouble. However, when Gloria first announced that we could expect a multiple birth, I wasn't exactly thrilled. The movie was taking longer than I had expected. Since Gloria was pregnant, I had sent her home with the boys.

"She telephoned me from the States at three A.M. She said that she had just learned that she was going to have twins—that her doctor had heard two heartbeats. I thought she was imag-

ining it since such a thing had never occurred to anyone in either
of our families.

" 'Go back to sleep,' I said. 'You were dreaming.' Then it hit
me that she was telling the truth. It was seven P.M. in California.
I wanted to rush right home, but she managed to calm me down.
Just as soon as the dawn came up, I dashed to the set. I just
had to tell someone the news. There was one man there—a very,
very practical Englishman. I told him about my call. In crisp,
businesslike tones, he said, 'Old chap, better drop in on Lloyd's
for some twin insurance.' The way he said it, brought me sharply
down to earth."

The children were used to seeing a steady stream of curious
tourist buses stop at their house so that passengers could catch
a glimpse of the Jimmy Stewart family. When the twins were
babies, their nurse would tell the sightseers, "This one sleeps
twenty-four hours a day; that one doesn't eat well." As Judith
and Kelly grew older, they joined their brothers in waving at
the rubberneckers.

"That's the least we can do," said eleven-year-old Michael.

And ten-year-old Ronnie added, "After all, they did pay a
dollar for a look-see!"

"Jimmy is a good companion to the children," said Gloria.
"He plays baseball and goes riding with them. The boys are
avid movie fans, but they're kind of fickle. For a long time their
favorite cowboy was Randolph Scott. It took me quite a while
to break them away."

The Stewarts tried to attend all parent–teacher meetings. This
often was difficult, since the children were enrolled at different
schools. "That didn't stop Jimmy from being darn proud of his
kids' scholastic achievements," recalled Mike Chaffey, the studio
electrician Stewart helped. "I'd show him pictures of my kids,
and he'd do the same. Only he always seemed to have lots more
of them. While I'd be admiring his pictures, he'd boast about
their latest accomplishments. Even those that backfired.

"Once when we were on location, he told me that his older

stepson's teacher had said the boy was improving greatly and was now the tenth smartest kid in class. 'That sure made me feel all puffed up,' Jimmy said. 'That's until I learned that the class only had eleven students!'

"He told me that now when he bumped into people they didn't just ask him about his current movie but inquired about the family. 'That's when I'd reach for my wallet,' he said, 'and take out my kids' latest pictures!' "

## CHAPTER XI

# THE FASTEST SLOWPOKE IN THE WEST

Over the years Jimmy made eighteen Western movies and loved doing every one of them. "In many ways, Westerns are the most legitimate and colorfully dramatic tales of Americana," he said. "Sure, there are some things that have been manufactured. But for the most part, those movies are pretty honest portrayals of what a wonderful part of our country was really like."

When, in 1972, Jimmy was elected to the Cowboy Hall of Fame, Walter Brennan, who was often cast as the loyal tobacco-chewing sidekick, remarked, "Jimmy Stewart's not one of your rootin'-tootin', quick-on-the-draw cowpokes. Ever since I saw him pin on the star in *Destry Rides Again*, I've been dang sure that in the long run he'd get the tinhorn gunslick that's been browbeatin' the town. Jimmy may look as if he's just dawdlin' along, but it ain't so. He's really one smart hombre. And straight as a hitching post!"

Undoubtedly, an overeager publicist prepared Brennan's statement, but it did reflect the sentiments of Stewart's friends and fellow actors. Their praise may have been less florid, but it was equally sincere:

Jay C. Flippen: "Nobody plays a cowboy better than Jimmy Stewart."

Rock Hudson: "He gives the Old West a good name."

Ward Bond: "Jimmy can be pushed just so far, then wham!"

Richard Widmark: "Jimmy, in his roles, makes up his mind slowly, but when he decides, he is resolute—no turning him around."

In addition to *Destry Rides Again* and *Broken Arrow*, many other of Stewart's movies about the settlement of the West are studied by college cinema classes as excellent examples of frontier films. Some of the plots may appear to be standard and trite—the hero never draws first and never resorts to unfair means in a hand-to-hand fight. Jimmy's acting, however, has turned some of them into minor classics; he is always the quietly determined person we should all like to be.

---

## WINCHESTER '73

Lin McAdam (Stewart) is a footloose cowboy in search of the man who murdered his father. On the fourth of July, 1876, McAdam enters the Dodge City Centennial Marksmanship Contest. He is declared the victor, defeating Dutch Brown (Stephen McNally), who is favored to win. McAdam's prize is a brand-new repeating rifle. He is one of the first westerners to own a Winchester '73—often called "the gun that won the West."

Anthony Mann, the director of the film, skillfully intertwined the movie around the rifle. It's stolen six times. The culprits are Brown, an Indian trader, an Apache chieftain, a fainthearted dude, a desperate outlaw and then back to Brown. McAdam learns that Dutch Brown is the man who killed his father. He retrieves the gun in a shootout on a mountaintop. There are six subplots, which kept everybody busy, and the movie established Stewart as a leading cowboy star. However, a television reviewer who recently saw the movie on the late show meanly called Jimmy "A sweet-tempered, stuttering Humphrey Bogart in chaps!"

# BEND OF THE RIVER

In this film, Stewart is cast as a former border rustler, Glyn McLyntock. He agrees to guide the wagon train of a band of farmers who are intent on reaching Oregon. Along the way, they encounter bandits and Indians. When a tribe of warring Shoshone braves attack the wagons, only McLyntock's heroism saves the scalps of the farmers and their families. He also outwits dozens of trigger-happy outlaws.

Arriving in Oregon, badly needed supplies intended for the farmers are stolen. McLyntock gets them back just as they are about to be sold to avaricious gold prospectors. He proves that he has truly reformed when he shuns the gold for the hand of pretty Laura Baile (Julia Adams), daughter of the farmers' leader.

"I always knew Glyn had character," she says after she accepts his proposal. "You can see it in his face."

# THE NAKED SPUR

Bounty hunter Howard Kemp (Stewart) arrives in Colorado seeking killer BenVandergroat (Robert Ryan). Kemp needs the reward money ($5,000) to buy back the farm he lost while he was away fighting in the Civil War. In the mountains, he meets an old prospector (Millard Mitchell) and a Union Army soldier (Ralph Meeker) who boasts about his dishonorable discharge. The three men discover Vandergroat and his female companion, Linda Patch (Janet Leigh), hiding out in a deserted shack. Vandergroat is captured.

Meeker and Mitchell want to share the reward. They decide to accompany Kemp back to Abilene where the bounty is to be paid. En route, Vandergroat tries to pit his three captors against each other. He also orders Linda to seduce Kemp. The greed-and-jealousy plans fail. Vandergroat, the prospector and the soldier are killed. Linda realizes that she has fallen in love with Kemp. (She hadn't done anything immoral; Vandergroat was just an old family friend.) She convinces Kemp to forgo the reward and instead they head for California to start new lives. Together, they ride off into the sunset.

## NIGHT PASSAGE

Whenever possible, Jimmy tried to play his accordion. James Neilson, the film's director, gave him the opportunity in this movie. Grant McLaine (Stewart) had been a trusted railroad detective, but because of a series of holdups, he is under suspicion. His boss, Ben Kimball (Jay C. Flippen), offers him one last chance to redeem himself. The train he's been assigned to guard is carrying a particularly heavy payload. McLaine hides the money with one of the young passengers, Joey Adams (Brandon de Wilde).

Again, the train is bushwacked by the same outlaws who committed the previous robberies. McLaine is captured. The gang leader, surly Whitey Harbin (Dan Duryea) brags about his newest recruit, the Utica Kid (Audie Murphy). The Kid is not only a superb marksman, but also McLaine's younger brother. The railroad detective plays melodies from earlier carefree days, hoping they will remind the Utica Kid of home and family. However, the accordion concertizing fails to awaken memories.

The outlaws are successful in locating the money. McLaine manages to break away, but he's soon trapped and is on the verge of being shot. Suddenly, the Utica Kid has a change of heart and throws in with his brother. Together, they defeat the desperadoes. The Kid is fatally wounded in the shootout but helps save the payload. McLaine is reestablished as a man who is loyal and dependable.

## THE MAN WHO SHOT LIBERTY VALANCE

This movie glorifies an era in a way that led a history professor from the University of Chicago to say, "John Wayne, James

Stewart and Hollywood combine to make the Old West live once more. Things may not have happened exactly that way, but secretly we all wish they did."

Jimmy plays distinguished U.S. Senator Rance Stoddard, who is a Presidential possibility. He is returning to Shinbone, Oklahoma, to attend the funeral of Tom Doniphon (John Wayne). A reporter asks him why he has traveled so far to be present at an inconsequential burial. Senator Stoddard relates an engrossing story about the man who is about to be laid to rest. "Without his help," he says, "I'd never have had a political career." (There is a flashback.)

Many years before, young Stoddard came from the East to practice law. At the time, Shinbone was threatened by a notorious killer named Liberty Valance (Lee Marvin). Only one man was not afraid of the outlaw—Doniphon. However, he refused to intervene.

Valance taunted greenhorn Stoddard into a gunfight. The lawyer had never handled a gun but felt he had to accept the challenge. The shootout occurred on a dark street. Valance fell dead from a bullet to the heart. The townfolk were so overjoyed they proposed to make Stoddard their first Congressman. He refused their nomination, saying that a man who had gained notoriety solely because of a killing should not receive such glory. At this point, Doniphon admitted that he had been hiding in the shadows and was the one who really did the shooting. But the legend lived on

In the closing scene, a train conductor bows and scrapes as he offers Stoddard a shiny new cuspidor. "Nothing's too good for the man who shot Liberty Valance," he says fawningly.

The Senator doesn't have to reply—his expression speaks for him. "Oh, what the heck!" he seems to be saying. Interspersed with the action leading to the final shootout, Stoddard talks about the importance of defending the small homesteaders from the attack of the cattlemen. "That was a case of democracy in action," Stewart said. "Westerns do that more readily than most other films."

81

## THE CHEYENNE SOCIAL CLUB

John O'Hanlan (Stewart), an aging bronco buster, has ridden the range so long he claims he's more swaybacked than his horse. "You gotta take better care of your mustang than yerself," he says in one of his talkative moods, "or else the whey-belly critter'd up and die on you."

The sagebrush philosopher's brother dies and leaves him a hotel in Wyoming. John invites his old partner, Harley Sullivan (Henry Fonda), to help him take possession of the legacy. Along the way, the two grizzled cowpokes engage in a memorable conversation:

HARLEY: I had a dog one time who used to lay on his back in the sun. Just lay there with his hind legs all spread out, you know, and his tongue hanging out of his mouth. He was laying there like that one day and a wagon ran over him. He never laid that way again. He always walked funny after that. He was a good dog, though Sam Breedlaw give him to me. Sam's married to my sister. He's a chamberpot and pin drummer . . .

JOHN: You know where we are now, Harley?

HARLEY: Not exactly.

JOHN: We're almost in the Wyoming territory. And you been talking all the way from Texas.

HARLEY: (injured) I've just been keeping you company.

JOHN: (restrained) I appreciate it, Harley, but if you say another word the rest of the day, I'm gonna kill you.

When they arrive in Wyoming, they discover that the hotel is actually a brothel, complete with a commanding resident madam and six willing scarlet women. The rest of the film is a satirical tale of bawdy innocence. O'Hanlan is incredulous. "Do you suppose this is a wh . . . ," he starts asking Sullivan. Then he suddenly stops and says, "Harley, you know exactly what I mean!"

The two old sidekicks also encounter a skinflint lawyer who wants to foreclose the bordello. They realize that all the "employees" have hearts of gold and have been bringing needed joy to the local male residents. With great ingenuity, John and Harley defeat the legal villain. Throughout the 103-minute movie, Stewart remains true to character—never once does he address the girls other than a polite "ma'am."

## THE SHOOTIST

When in 1976, Paramount asked the veteran actor to take a minor role in a movie starring John Wayne, he said he'd be honored. Stewart plays a frontier doctor who has to inform his old friend, a widely known gunfighter, that he is dying of cancer. Wayne demands to know all the gory details.

"Jimmy's grimacing and hand-twisting are memorable," said one reviewer. "Especially when he discloses to Wayne what to expect in the final hours. Any other actor would have wrecked that scene."

Many of the Hollywood cowboys had stand-ins do their riding and other hard stuff. Jimmy did it himself, to the extent his directors would let him. "He is a skilled horseman," said Anthony Mann, who directed him in eight movies. "Jimmy was always ready to do anything in the interest of realism.

"I'll admit, however, that he's a bit unorthodox. I guess it's easy to imitate the way he talks, but it sure is difficult to imitate the way he rides. Not only does he stay in the saddle on the orneriest four-legged critter, but he even makes the horse mighty pleased. I swear the horse looks back at him and smiles."

# CHAPTER XII

# HITCHCOCK'S ALTER EGO

"I made four movies with Hitch," Stewart said. "He had a way of bringing out the best in you. Almost challenged you to act. Once after doing a scene for him, he came over to me: 'Jimmy, that scene seemed very tired!' I realized exactly what he meant. Part of my problem has always been that I'm too slow. But he immediately knew how to handle it."

Stewart has often been referred to as "Hitchcock's alter ego"; the two worked very closely together from 1948 to 1958. "These days," Jimmy said, "we toss the word 'genius' around entirely too much, but he was a genius in the picture business. He had a quality all his own that I don't think will ever be found in a director again. Recently, there was a derogatory biography about him. It made me feel pity for the author. Hitch's personality, his morality, had nothing to do with his extraordinary skill."

Apparently, the legendary director of suspense thrillers felt the same way about the actor whom he called, "Unmatchable, but yet Mr. Everyman."

Grace Kelly, Stewart's co-star in Hitchcock's *Rear Window*, was well aware of the director's admiration for her lanky leading man. "Hitch rarely talked to the performers," she said. "But on the subject of Jimmy Stewart he seemed to be positively gabby.

Once, he was my dinner partner at my apartment in Paris. 'Jimmy and I have a lot in common,' he told me. 'He, too, is a painstaking craftsman. Critics concentrate solely on his boyish grin and halting delivery and ignore his superb acting ability. They have limited sight. Just watch the way he moves his hands and the rest of his body. Pay close attention to his eyes—a real professional!' "

In 1983–84, five of Hitchcock's movies were rereleased: *Rear Window*, *Rope*, *Vertigo*, *The Man Who Knew Too Much*, and *The Trouble With Harry*. For many years, they had been gathering dust because of legal restrictions. Stewart, who starred in four of the pictures, left his home in Beverly Hills to go to New York City to introduce them. "I've done many promotional tours in my day," he told the audience, "but this is sort of different because it's the second time around—and frankly, these movies have improved with age."

In his short introduction, he extolled their virtues, told why they were good and why they are enduring. The four Jimmy appeared in are:

---

## *ROPE*

---

Two young homosexuals (Farley Granger and John Dall) strangle a fellow student for the "thrill of it." The homosexuality was subdued considerably because of the Production Code of the time but not eliminated completely. Hitchcock admitted that part of the plot had been modeled after the unsavory Leopold and Loeb case.

The killers conceal the body in a chest in the parlor, where the victim's parents and girlfriend have been invited for cocktails. One of the other guests is their former philosophy professor (Jimmy Stewart), who has a reputation for being a Nietzsche scholar and for possessing a sharp and probing mind. The two youths are sure they can fool him. In a series of tantalizing clues, they hand him a stack of books that are tied together with the cord that was used for the murder; casually walk around the chest where they have hidden the corpse; carry on involved conversations about violent death.

At first, the professor appears to be gullible. He allows them to think he's been hoodwinked. The reviewer for the *Denver Post* said, "Early on, Stewart guesses what has happened, but he's people-smart and waits until he has all the evidence. Then he unravels the crime and alerts the police."

Hitchcock, who was both director and co-producer of the film, wanted Jimmy for the role of the professor. Stewart had recently returned from the war, and the financiers felt that he had been so long from public view that he was no longer good box office. They tried to convince Hitchcock to use another actor, but he persisted. Eventually, the money-men offered Jimmy $100,000, a sum calculated to make him refuse. He said he'd play the part free of charge for a percentage of the profit. They rejected his offer. Hitchcock obstinately insisted on Stewart for the role. Jimmy finally settled for $300,000.

"In *Rope* I didn't achieve the movie I hoped for," Hitchcock explained, "although it has remained one of my favorites. We had difficulties with lighting. This was my initial experience with color. But, as usual, Jimmy was notable. His facial expressions as he became suspicious were letter-perfect. Contrary to some of the reviewers, he doesn't have to rely on dialogue."

## REAR WINDOW

Stewart plays the part of a globetrotting news photographer who is confined to a wheelchair because of a broken leg. Bored by all the inactivity, he becomes a Peeping Tom. He uses binoculars to gaze in the courtyard windows that face his Greenwich Village apartment. Most critics lauded the movie but complained about his spying actions. Hitchcock defended his major character being a voyeur.

"What's so terrible about that?" the director asked. "Sure he's a snooper, but aren't we all? I'll bet you that nine out of ten people, if they see a woman undressing for bed, or even a man puttering around his room, will stay by the window and look."

One of the neighbors Stewart carefully studies is a traveling salesman (Raymond Burr). Jimmy is convinced that he has butchered his invalid wife. The audience is quickly caught up in Stewart's compulsive sleuthing. He maintains the viewer's sympathy even at his most querulous moments. However, he is unable to persuade his fiancée (Grace Kelly) and his detective friend (Wendell Corey) that a slaying has taken place. Jimmy becomes obsessed with trying to trap the killer. When he feels that he has gathered sufficient proof to confirm his suspicions, the murderer discovers that he is being watched and tries to kill him.

For side relief, Grace Kelly, a high-society fashion editor, attempts to seduce the incapacitated photographer into marriage. When she appears on the screen for the first time she stoops over him seductively and awakens him with a provocative kiss. She manages to appear both ethereal and full-blooded at the same moment. Stewart protests that she is "too perfect" and that "I'm not yet ready for marriage."

Most of the action takes place in Jimmy's living room. The windows that interest him the most reveal a variety of intimate scenes. They are like switching television channels idly: preoccupied newlyweds who pull their shades up and down; a very lonely lady who pours wine with a nonexistent suitor; a childless couple that lavish affection on a tiny dog that they lower up and down in a velvet-lined wicker basket.

The murderer is apprehended. But in the course of Jimmy's final deduction, his other leg is broken. "Pure Hitchcock!" Stewart remarked.

A story the director was fond of telling concerned an incident that occurred during the filming of *Rear Window*. "Somehow, a little old lady wandered onto the set," he said. "She was chased off several times, but persisted in traipsing back. I'm a bit of a ham. I have managed to play bit parts in many of my movies. In *Rear Window*, I was winding a clock with the cameras whirring, when she walked up and offered me the correct time. I became temporarily immobilized, then, I fear, I started reproving her

87

somewhat violently. That's when Jimmy ran over to her aid.
" 'Don't!' he shouted. 'She's probably someone's grandmother!' With that he put his arm around the old woman and
gently escorted her out. She accepted his chaperoning, but as
she left the set she stuck out her tongue at me. Jimmy did the
same!"

## THE MAN WHO KNEW TOO MUCH

The film was a remake of the 1934 Hitchcock movie of the same
name. In this one, Stewart plays a naive American tourist who
accidentally overhears plans for an international murder. He is
an exceptionally moral man and believes it's his solemn duty to
stop the killing. Before he succeeds, he gets into a mess of trouble.

Doris Day, who plays his wife, is a famous songstress. Her
rendition of "Que Sera Sera" helps him rescue their young son
from spies who discover that Jimmy knows their secret. The
closing scene set in London's Albert Hall is now regarded as
Hitchcock's masterpiece. The plan is to perform the killing during a concert; the assassin is to fire at the precise instant the
musical score calls for a clash of cymbals. With only seconds to
spare, Stewart subdues the murderer.

"That scene will stay with me for a long, long time," Jimmy
said. "When the assassination was about to take place, the orchestra was playing a symphony Hitch particularly liked. While
it was going on, Doris and I carried on a conversation sort of
explaining what was happening. Suddenly, Hitch appeared. 'You
two are talking so much that I can't enjoy the music!' he yelled.
'Cut out all the dialogue and act out the scene!'

"Doris thought he had gone bananas, but we did it his way.
The result was that the scene was twice as effective as it had
been before. And Hitch was able to enjoy the symphony without
interruption."

The plot was inspired by a real incident that involved Winston
Churchill when he was head of the British police force. "It seemed
some anarchists wanted to do away with a high government

official," Hitchcock explained. "A professor of European history from Oxford University told me about it. He claimed he had seen the movie eight times because of its eerie resemblance to the way it really happened. He said that each time he saw Jimmy stop the foul play from happening he nearly fell off his seat in 'awe and gratitude.' He told me that he always left the theater wanting to shake Jimmy's hand."

## VERTIGO

Scottie Ferguson (Stewart) is a detective who resigns from the San Francisco police department because of a severe case of acrophobia—a pathological dread of high places. He is hired by an acquaintance to shadow his moody wife (Kim Novak). The former detective falls wildly in love with the woman he is trailing. She attempts to drown herself. He saves her. She tries to kill herself again—this time she's successful. Because of his fear of heights, he is unable to rescue her when she throws herself off a tall church tower.

He is accused of having used his vertigo as an excuse for not following her closely enough. Overcome by guilt, he suffers a nervous breakdown. He keeps imagining she's still alive. One day he sees a woman closely resembling his dead lover. Only she's not really dead—she's very much alive—part of a bizarre hoax that has caused her to change identity so she can conceal a murder. He realizes that he has been the victim of a complicated deception.

"Only Hitchcock and Stewart could have made this complex whodunit believable," wrote the critic of a Boston newspaper. "There's an abundance of implausible coincidences, but with the master of suspense, they are quickly changed to a humanly plausible mystery of the first magnitude. There's plenty of mayhem and lust in this movie, but with Jimmy Stewart it's acceptable. With admirable realism he projects his fears and fantasies . . . The combination of Hitchcock and Stewart is unbeatable."

"Jimmy is a perfect hero," Hitchcock said, "because he is Everyman in bizarre situations. I mean, let's look at his private life—Princeton, Air Force General—he's not an uneducated oaf. You can believe him as a professor, a doctor, a family man. Just about anything."

Stewart was asked to comment on a provocative statement Hitchcock was supposed to have made: "All actors are cattle."

"I once asked Hitch about that," Jimmy recalled. "He denied it. 'I never said that,' he told me. 'What I actually said was, 'Actors should be treated like cattle.'

"As one of Hitch's cattle, I still believe he was great!"

# CHAPTER XIII

# HE SAVED HIS MONEY

"During the filming of one of my Westerns," Jimmy recalled, "I invited my parents to visit me on location. Dad watched me mount a horse. Then he said to my mother, 'Our boy climbs on that nag as if he's going to kiss it. He'll never get to the California gold fields that way.' "

Jimmy did—and struck pay dirt. He is reputed to be one of the wealthiest actors in Hollywood. But Stewart has never splurged on heart-shaped swimming pools or antique Rolls-Royces. Jack Benny, who lived nearby, called him "even more frugal than I am!" The comedian, whose trademark was parsimony, quipped, "Some people claim I'm stingy. Well, compared to Jimmy Stewart, I'm king of the big spenders. Not only does he have the first penny he earned, but the first penny his father gave him. And what's more, both coins are drawing interest!"

For most of Stewart's career, he was a leading box office attraction, causing Louis B. Mayer to remark in one of his unguarded moments, "With him in the picture we could usually look forward to making money. Not only for ourselves, but for him, too."

Jimmy's salary for appearing in a film was in excess of $250,000.

In 1950, when he was asked to make *Winchester '73,* his agent persuaded him to adopt a financial arrangement that has since been embraced by many stars—a percentage of the gross in lieu of a fixed salary. Jimmy gained more than $500,000 for that film and continued using the package-deal whenever possible.

A millionaire several times over, he has served on the boards of directors of several large corporations, with a partner in a charter airline service and owned oil wells. Currently, he has extensive real estate investments and a sizeable portfolio of stocks and bonds.

Guy Gadbois, Stewart's long-time business manager, said, "Most of Jimmy's investments have little relationship to the movie industry. But the most dissimilar venture was his ownership of a goat ranch. He'll long remember that one!"

"It started out innocently enough," Jimmy recalled. "At the time I was abroad making a film. Gadbois telephoned me overseas and reported that a highly lucrative Texas ranch was up for sale. He recommended that I buy it at once. Since I'd always taken his advice, I told him to go ahead. But I did ask what they did on the place. He said that it was a goat ranch with more than a thousand goats.

"With a few more transatlantic calls, I learned that goat's hair—known as mohair—was in great demand for upholstering couches and stuffed chairs. The hair grew so rapidly that the goats had to be clipped three times a year. Just as I was imagining myself as a mohair magnate, the market dried up due to foam rubber. Nobody wanted mohair, and the price fell to practically zero. I stored the mohair all over the place and had to rent dozens of large bins for the overflow. More clippings and more storage problems. But suddenly it became fashionable to make men's suits out of mohair. The price went up. Immediately, I told Gadbois to sell my ranch. To this day, whenever I see a man wearing a mohair suit, I want to walk up and shake his hand." The bulk of Jimmy's vast estate, however, comes from being an actor.

* * *

He was bored with playing the naive, bumbling, inarticulate hero who can do no wrong and demanded more variety in his characterizations. He got his wish. These roles resulted in even greater profits.

One of his outstanding successes, both artistically and commercially, was when he appeared in *Harvey* as the invisible six-foot rabbit's whimsical, usually inebriated companion, Elwood P. Dowd. For thirteen weeks, at Broadway's 48th Street Theater, Stewart played to standing room only. When, several months later, Universal International decided to turn the hit stage play into a movie, Jimmy was again asked to star. When Stewart won an Oscar nomination for the role of the gentle dipso, the studio decided to run advertisements that the film was "guaranteed to bring forth the happiest laughs you'll ever have."

"For once," said Jack Benny, "Hollywood underplayed a movie. Jimmy Stewart produced happy laughs in a warm and wonderful manner—and he laughed all the way to the bank!"

Some years later, Stewart returned to Broadway to appear in a revival of *Harvey*. For six weeks he once again was Elwood P. Dowd. "I've always loved the play," he said. "Always had it in the back of my mind that I'd like to do it again. I wasn't too satisfied with the movie version. I think I played him a little too dreamily. A little too cute-cute."

"Jimmy has never stopped expanding as an actor," said Alfred Hitchcock. "He usually has some new movements. Some new behavior. Watch him."

Jimmy continued to demand and be given offbeat roles. He played a chain gang convict in *Carbine Williams*. "Granted, it was a real change of pace," said Dave Chasen, a close friend and owner of an in-group Hollywood restaurant that Stewart frequented. "Despite the big change, audiences still thought of him as a nice, sweet guy. I'm sure it would be that way even if he robbed the mint or shot his plumber. His loyal fans would regard the actions as being quite proper—his name on the screen is enough to satisfy them. He doesn't even have to show his face for everyone to know it's going to be a decent movie."

In Cecil B. De Mille's film about the Barnum and Bailey circus, *The Greatest Show on Earth*, he did just that. "Throughout the film, he appeared in grinning, white-faced makeup as Buttons the clown," said Dorothy Lamour, who also had a part in the movie. "Few other big names would agree to completely hide their identity. But Jimmy felt so secure he did it willingly and had himself a great time."

"Can you imagine one of the movies' great profiles or lover boys wanting to be in a film in which the audience never sees his face?" director Henry Koster asked. "Yet, that kind of part is a challenge to Jimmy. He heard that De Mille was planning a circus picture in which there was a clown part. He called De Mille up and asked for the role. 'It's a very small part,' De Mille told him. 'And the clown never takes off his makeup.'

" 'Is the role essential to the plot?' Jimmy wanted to know. When De Mille answered 'Yes,' Jimmy said, 'It's a deal!' "

In the film, the clown costume conceals the identity of a famous physician who is sought by the police for murdering his wife— it was a mercy killing. In the melodramatic train crash finale, Brad, the circus owner (Charlton Heston), is seriously injured. Only an immediate blood transfusion can save his life. Buttons steps in and uses his medical skill, thus revealing who he really is.

The films Jimmy made drew mobs in three countries. Alfred Hitchcock, who directed him in four films, said, "Jimmy appearing in the film can mean at the very least another million dollars at the box office."

Of his popularity, Stewart said, "I tried to choose pictures that were acceptable for the whole family, not just for sophisticated and supposedly more intelligent adults. I looked for success stories, even in Westerns and thrillers—with characters worth developing."

In *Strategic Air Command*, another commercial success, Stewart came very close to playing himself on the screen. He was cast as a highly paid baseball star who sportswriters predicted would become one of the all-time greats. He is in the reserve and is suddenly called up to fly B-36 bombers in the peacetime Air Force. June Allyson plays his pregnant wife.

"As always," she said, "Jimmy's sincerity shines. He really believes that a citizen's duty is to come to the aid of his country."

One movie, however, was curiously a failure. For years, he had wanted to film the life story of Charles A. Lindbergh. Not only did Jimmy admire his flying, but he shared Lindbergh's conservative opinions. When *The Spirit of St. Louis* was about to be cast, Stewart volunteered to play the aviator, who was twenty-five years old when he made the solo flight across the Atlantic in thirty-three and a half lonely hours. Studio bosses felt that Stewart, forty-seven, was much too old for the role.

"I knew they wanted a younger actor," Jimmy recalled. "They didn't want to hurt my feelings, so they came up with the objection that I was too fat. Now I've been called many things in my time, but never too fat. Anyway, I was so determined to play Lindbergh that I went on a really tough diet. It paid off. After three weeks, they told me that I had the part, but at the same time, they asked me to stop dieting because I was beginning to look terribly ill. My face was gaunt, and I had black rings under my eyes."

Leland Hayward, who had become a producer, was the film's prime mover. "I've never seen such pestering," he said. "But what really made us finally give in was when Jimmy's widowed father came out to Hollywood on his honeymoon with his second wife he was eighty-four years old at the time!"

"After I was allowed to play the part," Jimmy said, "it was decided that it would be a good idea if we met with Lindbergh. He accepted the invitation. It was a great thrill for me. Shortly after his historic flight, he made a triumphant tour that brought him near my home. I'd always been a flying nut and hoped to get his autograph. But the crowds were so thick that I barely caught a glimpse of him. Bitterly disappointed, I returned home empty-handed.

"Now, years later, I still felt the same hero worship. I kept pinching myself that I was going to play the Lone Eagle. I still wanted Lindy's autograph, but I was too shy to ask for it."

95

Many Hollywood bigwigs were surprised when *The Spirit of St. Louis* failed to excite moviegoers. "It was a good film," Stewart said. "When the moment is right, I think someone ought to revive it. I've always considered it one of my best roles. I think I got right into Slim's character. I guess he thought so too. We became friends afterwards. I think the failure of the film was a great disappointment to him—one more jolt he had to take on the chin."

Jimmy received his fifth Oscar nomination for his portrayal of the defense lawyer in *Anatomy of a Murder*. Joseph Welch, the attorney who became famous during the McCarthy hearings, played the judge in the highly profitable movie. "It was uncanny the way Stewart handled the case," Welch said. "I had qualms about appearing in the movie, but he made me feel that I was actually presiding over a real trial. Although the case was all about rape, he didn't skirt the issue, but faced it square on. Yet he did it in a dignified fashion."

Otto Preminger directed the film. He, too, commended Stewart for making "a delicate plot acceptable." Jimmy plays a down-on-his-luck attorney who reluctantly agrees to defend an army lieutenant (Ben Gazzara) who is accused of murder. The lieutenant is charged with killing a man who raped his coquettish wife (Lee Remick). During the trial, Stewart had to match wits with the shrewd prosecuting counsel (George C. Scott).

Bosley Crowther, the dean of movie critics, reviewed the film for *The New York Times*. He called it, "The best courtroom melodrama I've ever seen . . . most brilliantly revealed is the character of the lawyer for the defense. Slowly and subtly, he presents us a warm, clever, adroit and complex man and, most particularly, a portrait of a trial lawyer in action which will be difficult for anyone to surpass."

At first, Jimmy's father didn't agree. Soon after it opened, he telephoned his son. "I understand you just made a dirty picture!" he bellowed.

"Where did you hear it?" Jimmy asked.

"A salesman came in and told me he saw the movie and that it was a damn, dirty, lousy picture," Alex shouted. "I'm going right over to the *Gazette* and put an ad in advising people not to see it!"

"And he did put an ad in," Jimmy recalled. "A year after the picture had been out it was playing in Homer City, about six miles from Indiana; he sneaked down and went to see it. He called me about three in the morning. 'I saw that dirty picture,' he said. 'I thought it was all right. You did a good job. But I don't see why you had to show the woman's panties.' "

Following *Anatomy of a Murder*, Jimmy appeared in two successive flops: Mervyn LeRoy's *The FBI Story* and Daniel Mann's *The Mountain Road*. LeRoy cast Stewart as Chip Hardesty, a veteran G-man who joined the bureau in its infancy. The two-and-a-half-hour documentary-style movie dealt with John Dillinger and Baby Face Nelson, the Ku Klux Klan, German espionage, spies, communists, oil-rich Osage Indians. A major part of the film, however, was concerned with Hardesty family affairs, turning it into a not very good soap opera.

In *The Mountain Road*, Jimmy plays a hard-bitten leader of a World War II demolition team. His assignment is to blow up bridges and roads in Southeast China, thus restraining Japanese troops. He carries out his orders, causing thousands of innocent Chinese to become homeless. His obdurate comment is, "Well, that's what war is all about." Eventually, he learns about benevolence and goodwill from a beautiful Eurasian woman. A reviewer for a Connecticut newspaper called the movie "two dimensional—silly and maudlin!"

Several months later, Jimmy was back on the winning track. This was difficult, since some of the major studios, claiming large financial losses, became too timid to try anything original. Remakes of old movies and duplication of former successes became routine. Nevertheless, Stewart was partially responsible for many box office triumphs. Among them were *The Man Who Shot Liberty Valance*, *Mr. Hobbs Takes a Vacation*, *Cheyenne Autumn* and *Shenandoah*.

*Mr. Hobbs Takes a Vacation*, which was made in 1962, was so successful that 20th Century-Fox tried repeating it twice in the following three years. They starred Stewart in *Take Her, She's*

*Mine* and *Dear Brigitte*. Although both imitations did moderately well at the box office, they fell short artistically.

"About the only thing that came out of those two lemons," said Jimmy, "was a very funny line in *Take Her, She's Mine*. John McGiver, an important member of the board of education, tries to tell me all of his troubles. That's when I reply, 'Telling me your troubles would be like complaining to Noah about a drizzle.'"

"I'm afraid," said Henry Koster, who directed the movies, "that was about all the humor those pictures had. It was too bad, because Jimmy has a definite flair for comedy. He played the harassed, long-suffering father brilliantly. But it was asking entirely too much of him to carry a well-hacked-over plot."

After switching between comedies and Westerns, Stewart was cast as Frank Towns, a grizzled bush pilot in Robert Aldrich's drama, *The Flight of the Phoenix*. Towns flies his rickety twin-engine transport over the Sahara Desert, conveying a bunch of oil company workers to a new site. The plane is destroyed when he is forced to crash-land. The remainder of the film is devoted to finding the best way of reaching civilization. Stewart didn't think it was a very good movie, yet reviewers lauded his performance. The film critic for *The Saturday Review* said, "It helps remind us what a splendid actor James Stewart really is."

Jimmy is very modest about his movie career. Not long ago, he said, "I've always felt that if you can act without letting it show—even if only for a few seconds—then you're home free."

In *Dear Brigitte* someone suggested that Stewart do a partially nude scene. "I'm much too old for that," Jimmy said. "And besides, no matter what they say, I'm too darn skinny. I look terrible without any clothes on. I wore tights in a picture called *Ice Follies of 1939*, and everybody said that they thought I looked awful. I was supposed to be a champion ice skater, but I wound up being the back half of a horse. Lew Ayres and I flipped for positions. I lost."

# CHAPTER XIV

# RON, HANK, GARY, DUKE AND JIMMY

In Hollywood, a community noted for heartache, jealousy and feuds, Stewart is not just liked, but well liked. Hundreds consider him their staunch friend. Four men unabashedly have loved him: Henry Fonda, Gary Cooper, John Wayne and Ronald Reagan.

"If I were marooned on a desert island," said Reagan, "and could choose a buddy to keep me company, there's never been any doubt who I'd pick. Jimmy Stewart knows when to talk, when to keep quiet, when to laugh and when to appear. I've been his friend for a long time and it's a privilege. I know that Hank and Gary and Duke felt the same way."

## HENRY FONDA

Stewart has frequently been described as a conservative Republican; Fonda, a liberal Democrat. "A long while ago, we agreed not to discuss politics," Jimmy said. "Our views never interfered with our feelings for each other. We just didn't talk about certain things. I can't remember ever having an argument with him—ever!"

"Jimmy is much too tenderhearted to be marked by any kind

of label," said Fonda. "He cares about people regardless of ideology or identity. He feels the same way about cats and dogs—he likes mixed breeds."

They met at Falmouth, Massachusetts, in 1932. Stewart, just out of Princeton, came for the summer. Fonda was playing leading roles for the University Players. "Jimmy just fell into acting," he said. "No training, no background. Me, I'd been at it, trying hard, for ten years. When I'd see him perform I'd think, 'What right has this green kid got to be so damn good?'

"He had the same gift that Marlon Brando had—the ability to speak lines naturally. Marlon did it years later, but people tend to forget that Jimmy did it first. I remember that when we were living together in New York, I tried to copy his style."

The first apartment they shared was a tiny railroad flat on 64th Street just off Central Park West. "At the time, we barely had toeholds on Broadway," Jimmy recalled. "High rent was out of the question. To help us share costs, two of our other friends moved in with us: Josh Logan and Myron McCormick. We formed a barbershop quartette—our big number was harmonizing on "Sam, the Accordion Man." The singing helped keep our minds off the dismal living quarters.

"Most of the other tenants in the building were hardworking prostitutes. Hank told me they appreciated good music, especially my accordion playing. Whenever I practiced, he'd run up to me and say, 'The girls are rapping on the walls. They're demanding more.' When they weren't enjoying my accordion playing, they were busy at work. It was impossible to leave our apartment without stumbling into a satisfied customer."

Policemen frequently raided the house and the building next door, which was a haven for gangsters—among them Legs Diamond. One evening, as Stewart and Fonda were leaving for the theater, they were stopped by their excited janitor who told them that if they had come out a few minutes earlier, they would have witnessed a real gangland slaying right on the front steps.

"Living there literally was a pistol," Jimmy said. "When our lease ran out, we decided to move."

They selected two rooms at the Madison Square Hotel. "It was convenient to Broadway theaters," he said. "Both Hank and I had landed roles in a play called *All Good Americans* written by the humorist S. J. Perelman and his wife. We figured that with steady salaries coming in we could afford something classier. The new bedroom actually had a window in it."

Unfortunately, the new show was not successful and closed after a short run. A notice posted on the theater bulletin board announced that the final performance would be given on New Year's Eve. Alongside the bad news was an invitation to attend a *"farewell party to help drown your sorrows."*

Stewart brought along his accordion. The downhearted company drank cheap red wine and sang dirgelike songs. The party broke up at four A.M. Instead of taking the subway home, the two mellowed actors decided to walk. When they reached Times Square they stumbled into a derelict who was trying to get to sleep on the sidewalk. Jimmy reached for his accordion and played "Rock-a-by Baby." Soon several vagrants had gathered and Stewart accepted requests. The two favorites were "A Shanty in Old Shanty Town" and "Brother, Can You Spare a Dime?" At the conclusion, Fonda passed the hat. Jimmy says nine cents was collected. Fonda disagreed. "He's always exaggerating," he said. "It was only six cents."

As they were preparing to leave, a very angry policeman appeared. "What do you think you're doing?" he shouted. "I get these people bedded down for the night, and you come along and wake them up! Now, it'll take me the rest of the night to get them back to sleep! Scram before I run you in for disturbing the peace!"

Some weeks later, Stewart was given a part in *Divided by Three*, which starred Katherine Cornell. To celebrate, he and Fonda, both jazz devotees, went to an East 52nd Street nightclub that prided itself on having "the hottest combo in town." Again, Jimmy brought his accordion. "It seemed that it went along everywhere," Fonda said. "Jimmy was so carried away by the music that he tried to sit in with the band. They kept chasing him away, but he wouldn't take no for an answer. Finally, the bouncer had to give him the old heave-ho. But even being tossed out didn't stop Jimmy. He made us wait until the musicians came out at closing time. Right there on the street he pestered them to join him. They did. Humoring Jimmy, I feel sure, so they could get him out of their hair."

When Stewart and Fonda both found themselves in Hollywood, they decided to resume their living arrangement. They rented a small Mexican-style farmhouse in Brentwood. Their next-door neighbor was Greta Garbo. They wanted to meet the beautiful Swedish actress who had made it clear that she desired complete privacy.

"We tried conventional methods like ringing her doorbell armed with roses," Jimmy said. "A uniformed maid would always answer with the stock reply: 'Miss Garbo is indisposed!' We spent hours plotting ways to sneak a look at her. One night, we got drunk and started digging a tunnel that led to her yard. We rehearsed what we'd say when we met her: 'Hi, honey. We have no ulterior motives. We just want to see you in your long, lean flesh.' We quit digging when we hit a water main."

Fonda insisted that the story wasn't exactly true. "Jimmy is a great storyteller," he said. "He embroiders a yarn. I was always the innocent party to his shenanigans. He kept getting me into all kinds of predicaments. Even the housekeepers he employed for us were out of this world. One maid had a notion that it was part of her job to see that we got eight hours of sleep. When we had guests, she'd appear at the stroke of ten carrying the visitors' hats and coats. Then she'd glare at them until they got the hint. Another felt it was her bound duty to censor all our dates. If she thought the girl's telephone voice sounded too sexy, she'd forget to deliver the message."

Fonda and Stewart often double-dated. "We'd take the girls to the Coconut Grove or the Trocadero," Jimmy recalled. "Many celebrities were regular customers. They just got up and entertained. Mary Livingston and Jack Benny, Gracie Allen and George Burns. One night, Judy Garland came in with her mother. All of us applauded. Judy took a bow and sang more than a dozen numbers. Red Skelton did his routine of pantomines. Bob Hope kept us laughing with his one-liners. Hank laughed so hard, he split his pants."

Stewart made no secret of his grief when Fonda died. "I've just lost my oldest and dearest friend," he said.

---

## GARY COOPER

---

Jimmy and Gary were known as two of Hollywood's less garrulous stars. They avoided long-winded conversation. "Or for that matter," said Frank Capra, "any conversation at all. They often communicated solely by using hand and head gestures. That didn't stop Coop from telling me, 'I so enjoy talking to Jimmy.' "

Capra, who had directed both of them in memorable movies— *Mr. Deeds Goes to Town* (Cooper) and *Mr. Smith Goes to Washington* (Stewart)—recalled, "One morning I was watching Jimmy mow his lawn when Gary drove over. They waved greetings. Then Coop raised his hands and made some shooting signs. Jimmy nodded. Coop held up two fingers. Jimmy shook his head. Instead, he raised three fingers. This time it was Gary who was negative. He held up four fingers. Jimmy nodded; Coop nodded. Friday—four days away. Nothing had been said. Nevertheless, an invitation to go hunting had been made and accepted. They waved goodby as Coop drove away."

When not silent, they were succinct. Writer Maurice Zolotow reported, "They once went out for a long walk in the woods. Suddenly, a large bird flew overhead. Cooper raised his hand and fashioned a gun. 'Bang!' he said. Stewart looked up admiringly. 'Good shot, Gary,' he said. They continued their walk in silence."

Jimmy still retains his faith in lucid stillness. "The problem with our country these days," he recently observed, "is that everyone is talking so darn much." His advice: "For one thing, lowering our voices would help a lot. If we don't, I'm afraid we're going to shout the country to death."

Sam Wood, a film director known for his deft skill with baseball scripts, was indebted to them. They starred in two of his distinguished films: *The Pride of the Yankees* (Cooper) and *The Stratton Story* (Stewart). He said, "Those two are admired for their ability to project quiet intensity and personal integrity." Then he added, "Plus a strong touch of shrewd parsimony. It is for real. They both know where every dollar goes."

Nora Sayre, writing in *The New York Times*, discussed their similarity. She wasn't too complimentary. "The male naif, as embodied by Gary Cooper and James Stewart, is a startling and even rather disturbing phenomenon when currently inspected . . . Granted, that goodness used to be popular, and the rustic who triumphs over the treacheries of the city is an American favorite, the fact that Cooper and Stewart persisted seems quite amazing today." She quoted such lines as: "I'm just a simple guy still wet behind the ears," and "Gee whiz, I'm still mixed up."

Pete Martin, another writer, disagreed. Martin, who wrote several articles about Cooper and Stewart for *The Saturday Evening Post*, said, "Those two expressed sentiments in their movies that are badly needed today. Over and over they demonstrated that goodness triumphs over evil. And what's wrong with a Norman Rockwell outlook? I remember Jimmy telling me, 'Coop's belief in candidness and integrity is still our best hope.' "

In April of 1961, Gary was given a special Oscar for his "stellar contribution to the cinema." Battling cancer, he was unable to accept the award in person. Stewart was his selected substitute. As Jimmy received the statuette, he whispered, "We're all very proud of you, Coop. All of us are very proud . . ." He couldn't go on and stumbled back to his seat.

A reporter once asked Cooper for the name of his best friend. The usually reticent actor, who was seven years older than his equally constrained co-worker, snapped: 'The new Gary Cooper— Mr. James Stewart! Who else?'

# *JOHN WAYNE*

A genealogist claimed that Wayne and Stewart were related: "Duke's great-great-aunt by marriage was Jimmy's first cousin once removed."

"I can't rightly figure it out," Stewart said, "but if it makes me any closer to Duke, it's pretty darn good . . . Whenever I got discouraged about the movie business, I'd think of him and thank my lucky stars that he was part of it."

When Jimmy received an Oscar for his role in *The Philadelphia Story*, Wayne was one of the first people to congratulate him. "It couldn't happen to a nicer guy," he told Stewart. "And a guy who just happens to be a hell of an outstanding actor. The movie industry sure was damn smart to give it to you!"

Twenty-nine years later, Jimmy had an opportunity to reciprocate. He did it in typical Stewart style. "I was watching the Academy Award show in a hotel," he recalled. "It was announced that John Wayne won the Oscar for Best Actor. I jumped up and down, whistled and yelled. The people next door called the manager, complaining that I was making too much noise. But I didn't care. I sat right down and sent Duke a wire:

YOU'VE BEEN A TREMENDOUS ASSET TO THE PICTURE BUSINESS FOR AN AWFUL LONG TIME. TONIGHT, YOU SAVED THE PICTURE BUSINESS. P.S. THE INDUSTRY WAS SMARTER THAN EVER WHEN THEY GAVE IT TO YOU. P.P.S. I'M MIGHTY PROUD TO BE YOUR FRIEND.

"We both made pictures for John Ford," Stewart said. "He is one of greatest directors of all time. Really knows his business, that is except for hats. He wanted me to wear a large sombrero that Duke had worn in all of his Westerns. I wanted my own favorite. It had become a good luck omen to me. I showed it to Ford. He took it, tossed it on the ground and jumped on it several times.

"'Now try it on,' he ordered. When I put it on, he examined it from every angle. 'Well, all right,' he said grudgingly. That meant, as I found out later, my hat would do for big outdoor shots, but I was still supposed to wear Duke's hat in all the town shots."

"Lucky it was only my hat," Wayne joked when he heard the story. "What if it had been my boots? I've got darn big feet!"

"That would have been out of the question," Jimmy said. "Nobody, but nobody, could possibly fill Duke's shoes. He may have been far from perfect. Sure, he made his mistakes as I have and you have. But, all in all, I would say they were unintentional mistakes of the heart. He was an original—a statue of his time."

---

## RONALD REAGAN

---

When Reagan became governor of California there was immediate talk of his being excellent material for higher office. This started a widely quoted gag that made studio rounds: A script is being cast. The producer says, "Ronnie for the President."

"Hell, no!" replies the director. "Jimmy Stewart for President. Ronnie for his best friend."

Stewart and the President of the United States have been close companions for many years. Reagan claims Jimmy was partly responsible for his entering politics. "I very much wanted a movie role that instead went to him," Reagan said. "I so wanted to be loaned to MGM to star as the one-legged baseball pitcher in *The Stratton Story*. When Jimmy landed the part, I was so disappointed, I began thinking of other fields."

The two men were active spokesmen for conservative political groups on the West Coast. When, in 1966, Reagan was the California Republican gubernatorial candidate, Jimmy lent both his moral and financial support. "He's one of us," Stewart told a Hollywood fund-raising party. "With Ron at the helm, our state will be in secure hands." The support continued when Reagan sought the presidency in 1976.

It wasn't Jimmy's first venture into presidential politics. Four years before, he introduced Pat Nixon at the Republican convention. "He did a terrific job," Richard Nixon said. "You'd almost think Pat was the candidate by the way he listed her virtues. When Pat was an aspiring actress, she once appeared with him in a movie called *Small Town Girl*. She only had a bit part, but to hear him describe it, it sounded as if she was the star. I don't mind telling you that Pat was thrilled by the eloquent introduction."

Once again, in 1980, Jimmy's familiar face was seen at Republican political rallies. An active role in the campaign had to be curtailed because of a bout with typhoid fever. When Reagan uttered the memorable line in the New Hampshire primary: "I paid for the microphone," Stewart clapped his hands and roared out his glee.

"That does it!" he said happily. "Ron will be our next President!"

At Stewart's seventy-fifth birthday party in Indiana, Pennsylvania's town square, Reagan called him from the White House. The telephone was hooked up to the loudspeaker. Just as Jimmy said, "Ron, I mean Mr. President," two Air Force jets screamed overhead and dipped their wings in tribute. Reagan had ordered them to salute his old friend. The planes made four passes, drowning out the conversation.

"Can't you hear me, Jimmy?" Reagan asked.

"That was some of your defense, Sir," Stewart replied. "And they looked awfully good."

Although the two men have never appeared together in the same movie, they are minutely sensitive and responsive to one another's film careers. Reagan has said, "Jimmy is a one-of-a-kind star. God threw away the mould when He made him."

And Jimmy returns the compliment. "Ron's acting ability has not been appreciated," he said. "It's grossly underrated. His portrayal of an amputee in *King's Row* was one of the great ones."

Stewart has complete confidence in Ronald Reagan. Evidently, Reagan feels the same way about him. He was recently asked about the friendship. "Let me tell you about that man," he replied. A half-hour later he was still raving. He was interrupted by an aide who reminded him that he had to attend a very important meeting. Reagan apologized for having to call a halt to the discussion about Stewart. "I've only begun to scratch the surface," he said sadly. "I could go on forever talking about that man."

# CHAPTER XV

# "YOU'RE A NATURAL FOR TV"

Many movie stars have gone into television because of promises of earning easy money. "You work a few hours a week and watch the green stuff roll in," their agents keep telling them.

Jimmy always refused. He had previously been a guest on talk shows and quiz programs, had sparred with Jack Benny, dropped in on Dean Martin and chatted with Dinah Shore. But to all offers that he do a weekly series, his answer was a firm "NO!"

He also made a number of TV appearances on leading dramatic shows. "As long as it isn't a regular thing," he said, "I'm happy to participate." One of the more enjoyable video performances was when he starred in an original *GE Theater* play cast as an aging cowboy in a Western version of Charles Dickens's *Christmas Carol*. "That show drew hundreds of rave notices," recalled Ronald Reagan. "I was host of the program. Viewers wrote in from all parts of the country. I remember one letter we received from a general store owner in Maine. 'I used to out-Scrooge Scrooge,' the man wrote. 'That was until I saw Jimmy Stewart. Not only did he turn me completely around, but I went right out and bought presents for just about everybody I knew!' "

Another performance that gave Stewart great pleasure was when he was a mystery guest on *What's My Line?* The panel,

Dorothy Kilgallen, Arlene Francis and Bennett Cerf, were blindfolded before they tried to identify the visiting celebrity.

"That was one of the high points in my life when host John Daly announced that I had stumped the experts," Jimmy said. "For years, people have easily recognized my voice. It got to be the stock in trade to mimic me. So it was no wonder that I tried to mask my identity."

Stewart thinks that Sammy Davis, Jr., does the imitation best. At one Hollywood party they both attended, the guests enjoyed a conversation between the real Jimmy Stewart and the pretender. "It was so good," Jimmy said, "that I had trouble picking out the authentic one."

Later, Cerf said, "I may not be as good as Sammy Davis, but I could always count on sure laughs when I copied Jimmy's high-pitched and hesitant drawl. But this time he had me fooled. When he realized he had succeeded, he jumped up and down with glee. I've rarely seen somebody so ecstatic. I told him that it would be fun to see him perform every week."

Fred MacMurray, whose series *My Three Sons* was continually in TV's top-ten shows, also urged Jimmy to think seriously about a regular program. "I told him repeatedly," said MacMurray, an old friend, "that with his talent for comedy and his vast following, he'd be a natural for television."

Jimmy, at length, bought it—disastrously. "I guess if there's where the action is," said the sixty-three-year-old actor, "I'll have to give it a try. It seems that everyone has a movie theater in the living room."

Stewart's first attempt was criticized severely. In the 1971–72 season, NBC agreed to pay him $35,000 a week to play the leading role in a half-hour domestic situation comedy called *The Jimmy Stewart Show*. He played an absentminded anthropology professor who was known for his constant good nature. The professor became a father and grandfather at the same time. The story line was built around the problems that can beset four generations who try living under the same roof: the professor, his wife, mother-in-law, thirty-year-old son, daughter-in-law, five-year-old grandson and five-year-old son. *The New York Times* called the series "heavy with integrity. Unfortunately, it is even heavier with banality and boredom."

When it folded, Jimmy refused all interviews. The word was that he was forever disillusioned with television. Some months later, he decided to speak out. Unlike other performers who heap the blame on the producer, director and writer, he accepted all the faultfinding. "I had too much authority," he told Marilyn Beck, a widely syndicated Hollywood columnist. "And I made too many errors. I was given approval of all the characters, the scripts, the shooting schedule. It just didn't work. People should stick to what they do well. I'm an actor. Someone else should have been calling the shots."

He emerged from the sad experience a somewhat wiser man. When, a year later, CBS asked him to star in *Hawkins*, a miniseries modeled after his movie role in *Anatomy of a Murder*, in which he was a lawyer, he was interested. But he insisted that more knowledgeable television heads do the bossing.

This time the casting was good. He played Billy Jim Hawkins, an elderly criminal attorney, who was folksy, foxy and capable of producing the surprising last-minute courtroom drama that TV writers seem to feel is an absolute must. (He always won his case.) Billy Jim Hawkins was a bachelor. His assistant and constant companion was his cousin, whose hick, back-country style tended to make the lawyer look almost sophisticated. Almost! Several times each episode Billy Jim still was required to utter "Aw, shucks!"

*Hawkins* was a tremendous success. Jimmy explained why: "When the facts were against me, I argued the law. When the law was against me, I argued the facts. And when the facts and the law were both against me, I banged my hands on the table. That formula seemed to work—convincing on TV, at least."

Home audiences and the critics liked the show. This time *The New York Times* called it, "The most impressively acted, written, directed and photographed of the new series so far this year."

In 1974, Jimmy won the Golden Globe Award for Best Actor

in a Dramatic Series. David Karp, the show's creator and producer, said, "Billy Jim is more than a lawyer—he is the older brother, the uncle, the father we all wanted. I created him because he was the kind of man I would have liked to have known in real life—whether he was a lawyer, a doctor, a judge, a teacher, a cop or a storekeeper. In short, he's Jimmy Stewart!"

"I enjoyed playing Hawkins," Jimmy said. "But I sure had to memorize a lot of lines. It seems that lawyers talk a blue streak. That's why Westerns were such a comfort to make— cowboys don't talk much. I was once asked to do *Winchester '73* on the old Lux Radio Theater. They wanted to broadcast a radio version of it. But when they saw all the blank pages in the script they got cold feet. There wasn't enough dialogue in that two-hour film to fill fifty minutes of radio time."

Much of the shooting on *Hawkins* was done on an MGM lot Jimmy had often worked on during his film career. He'd sit in his canvas-backed director-type chair and reminisce about earlier days. "I don't want to sound like some cornball old-timer who insists the old days were better," he said, "but I guess I still believe in sentimentality. I still like to make moviegoers cry. There were fewer stories of hopelessness and frustration.

"I wish today's young actors would laugh a little more. I wish they would not take themselves as seriously as they do. Some of the young people I've worked with just didn't seem to have fun in their craft. They were undisciplined and selfish; they seemed to be almost self-conscious in scenes. More interested in getting into tight-fitting jeans than getting into the character they were playing.

"How I wish there were more humor. When I got started, right in the heart of the Depression, the theater was a bright, gay, lively, enthusiastic place, and the young people had fun. Now, at age twenty-one, they are concerned about what to do when they grow old.

"Oh, sure, getting older means adjustments. A leading man who is known for his ardent wooing of the ladies, has to shop around for character parts. It's even tougher for actresses. The camera is especially unkind to the lady who has passed middle-age. The one exception is Katharine Hepburn—she has permanent beauty.

"I guess I was plain lucky to come to Hollywood when I did. At the time, it was a wonderful training ground for young actors. I don't think television has filled the gap. TV simply doesn't offer a youngster the varied roles and experience you need to learn your craft. But there I go being a cornball old-timer."

Maurice Zolotow, a veteran Hollywood writer, visited him during one of the *Hawkins* episodes. "Jimmy spoke with love and reverence of the old studio," Zolotow said. "He feels that we should disregard the clichés about MGM being a factory. 'The Metro executives were not power-drunk tyrants,' he told me. 'Actors were treated very well. You were employed fifty-two weeks a year. And they took you under their wing. They protected you if you got in a scrape. They fixed your teeth and got you new clothes and took care of your publicity. In my case, they told me I had to put on some weight and they sent me to their bodybuilder.' "

Jimmy has strong thoughts about studio loyalty. He had once appeared in court as a character witness for Sam Goldwyn. The fabled cinema high priest was being sued for reneging on an oral contract. "Mr. Goldwyn has been a friend of mine for years," Jimmy told the court. "In all that time, I've never known him to break his word."

Goldwyn was very moved. Known for his fractured semantics, he said, "To be thought of like that by Jimmy Stewart is the tallest compliment a person could probably have. It's almost as tall as he is himself. Jimmy will be a giant star as long as he lives or as long as I live!"

Late in 1983, Stewart and Bette Davis appeared in a television production, *Right of Way*. They played an elderly married couple who discover that the wife is dying from an incurable disease. They decide that life without the other would be unbearable, and methodically plan a joint suicide. Jimmy tries to explain his plan to their unmarried daughter, "We've lived to-gether . . . we're going to die together."

"At age seventy-five," one reviewer wrote, "Stewart still retains his stuttering patterns that made him a prime target for impersonators, and he still uses them with remarkable skill."

When Bette Davis saw the early scenes, she exclaimed, "There are four remaining superstars: myself, Cagney, Hepburn and Jimmy." About Stewart she added, "And he's the nicest!"

# CHAPTER XVI

# "DREAM FACTORY'S OUTSTANDING MARRIAGE"

Most people in "show biz" have been married a lot more than once: Zsa Zsa Gabor—eight times, Elizabeth Taylor—seven, Lana Turner—seven, Mickey Rooney—eight. For thirty-five years, Jimmy Stewart has had one wife and gets euphoric when he speaks of her. A fan magazine, notorious for its harsh treatment of Hollywood couples, recently called the Stewart union "Dream Factory's outstanding marriage."

"I once asked Jimmy about the quality of his marriage," said Frank Capra. "He was silent for a few minutes," said the director. "Then he scratched his ear and drawled, 'It's good . . . Darn good . . . I guess it's that way because Gloria and I really like each other . . . and we're not afraid to show it.'"

During those thirty-five years, the Stewarts have experienced some grievous moments brought on by illness, death and disappointment. But never by the sexual scandals that are so commonplace in the film capital. "On the whole, it's been a darn wonderful life," Jimmy said. "I've had so many blessings and good fortune. Gloria and the children continue to bring me enormous pleasure."

Daughter Kelly has a doctorate in zoology. Like her mother, she has always been interested in wildlife. Kelly's husband is

115

also a zoologist. The couple live in England, where both are teaching. "They met in Ruanda, Africa," said Jimmy. "Kelly was studying mountain gorillas. I visited her there. Right off, I discovered that I was too old for those frisky gorillas. Hairy things with long arms that kept pounding their chests. They weigh about 800 pounds apiece. Once, I was focusing my camera near a clump of trees, when six feet from me, I noticed this gorilla. Now, he wasn't doing much. Just staring. I kind of stared back. It's a good thing I had fast film. But Gloria and I like the brush. We've gone on a number of safaris."

Jimmy's other daughter, Judy, was an English major at Lewis and Clark College in Portland, Oregon. She is married to an investment banker. Together with her husband and two young children, she lives in San Francisco. "Judy's a fine writer," Stewart said. "From the time she was a little girl, she was interested in words. She's responsible for broadening my reading habits. For several years she worked in a game lodge in Tanzania. But that didn't stop her from reading the latest books."

Michael is married and the father of two children. He teaches economics in a Phoenix, Arizona, high school. "To hear Jimmy speak about his grandchildren," said Capra, "those kids have to be the greatest and best looking in the world. He whips out their pictures faster than a TV screen displays film credits."

Stewart's other stepson died in Vietnam. As soon as Ronald graduated from Colorado State, he enlisted in the Marines. Eleven days before his twenty-fifth birthday, the young lieutenant was killed in action as he was leading a patrol. He encountered Vietcong soldiers and died instantly from a machine gun blast.

At the time, Jimmy was in Santa Fe, New Mexico, filming *The Cheyenne Social Club* with Henry Fonda. "When the news came that Ronnie was dead," said Fonda, "Jimmy seemed to stop talking. Oh, he'd know his lines all right, but that was about all he'd say. How he was attached to that boy—helped raise him since he was five years old. Jimmy would disappear after a take. You could usually find him in the corral staring at the horses."

When Stewart was asked if Ronald's death in Vietnam was

116

wasted, he replied, "No! No! Our son didn't die in vain. His mother and I are proud that he served his country. When he got on the field of battle, he conducted himself in a gallant manner. We don't look at it as a tragedy. The tragedy was that our boy and so many like him were sacrificed without having a unified country behind them."

For more than two decades, Jimmy served in the U.S. Air Force Reserve. Each year, he put on his uniform and spent two weeks being briefed and flying some of the latest planes. He was an official observer on a bombing mission over Vietnam. "I piloted the aircraft," he said, "but didn't take part in the actual bombing." A typical two-week tour had him hopping around from Colorado Springs to Washington to Hawaii to Cape Kennedy before returning to Hollywood.

In 1957, the Armed Services Committee considered elevating him to general. Senator Margaret Chase Smith, Republican of Maine, strongly opposed the move. In a statement that was widely reported, she said, "I personally like Jimmy Stewart, the actor, as do thousands of his loyal admirers. I probably sound like a villainess to them, but popularity shouldn't be the yardstick by which we promote officers."

The rumor was that her protest stemmed from the fact that her administrative assistant, William C. Lewis, Jr., who was also a colonel in the Air Force Reserve, had been omitted from the list. By a vote of eleven to two, the committee rejected Stewart's promotion.

For several weeks, it was leading news. Jimmy refused to attack Senator Smith. "I guess she's wrong," was as far as his criticism would go. Instead he told reporters, "I was honored to receive the nomination by President Eisenhower and the Air Force. I intend to continue to do my best and fulfill my duty." Twenty-three months later, he was renominated and raised to one-star rank.

Upon his retirement in 1968, Jimmy received the Distinguished Service Medal. It was only the second time it had been awarded to an Air Force reserve officer. The citation read:

> The singularly distinctive accomplishments of General Stewart culminate a long and distinguished career in the service of his country and reflect the highest credit upon himself and the U.S. Air Force.

Jimmy likes to be called general. "Some of my proudest and happiest moments were spent in the Air Force," he said. "But the whole attitude toward the military concerns me very much. There are forces today, and where they come from I don't know— probably from within and without—they are trying to soil the image of the military. It's disturbing to see these forces try to discredit the military and send it back into isolation like it was after World War I. I think the armed forces contain some of the finest people in our country today—the professional military person. I spent twenty-seven years in the military, and it meant a great deal to me in life. I know that the principles and standards I learned made me a better civilian."

For a good part of his adult life, Stewart had served on the Los Angeles executive board of the Boy Scouts of America. Regardless of a heavy filming schedule, he usually found time to take an active role. "I think a lot of grownups refuse to participate," he said, "because they are afraid people will laugh at seeing a mature person in a Scout uniform. Actually, it makes me feel good to put one on. When I say that I get more out of Scouting than I put in, it may sound like a cliché, but it's true! I wouldn't trade my experience in Scouting for anything. Kids are just plain wonderful!"

"I was present when Jimmy Stewart gave a talk to the Los Angeles Area Scout Council a few years back," said Ken Henning, a podiatrist. "Frankly, I didn't want to attend, but my wife felt it would demonstrate to our two young sons that we cared. So, to please her, I went. But the truth is that I'm damn tired when I come home. I want to relax. Certainly not volunteer to be a Scoutmaster as my wife suggested.

"Stewart did hand out some unadulterated crap at the start.

118

But even then, he sounded so sincere that he got to me. When he said something about a man who was a Scout in his youth and was a better person because of it and that the world was a better place because of the Scout movement, it really did it.

"Yeah, I signed up!"

"It's routine for a celebrity to pay courtesy calls on a very sick child," said Paul Goodson, a New York City advertising executive. "I know the routine. It happened to me when I was eight years old. My picture appeared in all the newspapers after I suffered third degree burns in a sensational fire. I helped rescue my younger sister. Dozens of big names came to see me—even Babe Ruth and Clark Gable. Mayor La Guardia presented me with a scroll for my bravery. The procedure rarely varied. The VIPs would shake my hand—my left hand. It was the only part of my body that wasn't swathed in bandages; a photographer would record the event, followed by a hasty exit.

"Then came Jimmy Stewart with the usual photographer on hand. But after they snapped the picture, Jimmy remained behind. He had brought me an airplane model kit, but soon realized that I couldn't handle it. When he spotted a Ouija board my grandmother had given me, he fashioned a turban out of a towel and proceeded to tell my fortune. We talked and laughed a great deal. Jimmy came back two more times. Both times without a photographer!"

Peter Fonda also recalled visits of his father's closest friend. "Our house seemed to be Jimmy's second home," Peter said. "He was there all the time. How Jane and I looked forward to his appearance. He didn't treat us like most of the other adults— that we were little children who didn't know anything. Jimmy Stewart didn't talk down to us. You instinctively knew he was pleased to be with us."

John Ford, who directed him in *Cheyenne Autumn*, said much the same thing: "Jimmy has the wonderful quality of making you aware that he's happy to be in your midst. Other actors feel they're doing you a favor by just showing up. Not he!"

Stewart was asked if any of the directors he worked with had a great influence on his career. Jimmy was reflective. Then said,

"I think Frank Capra had, very definitely. Hitchcock has. John Ford very definitely. Henry Hathaway. Henry Koster is another. Tony Mann . . . I guess all those I worked with. I've been fortunate to have worked with the best."

Koster was flattered but not too surprised that he was included. "That's Jimmy for you," he said. "He really means it. He's like Will Rogers—I don't think he's ever met a man he didn't like. Once in a picture we were making, a member of the cast was widely known for his explosive temper. The slightest thing would set him sizzling like a roman candle. During the shooting, he got into dozens of squabbles. It got so bad that no one would talk to him—that is, no one but Jimmy. The other cast members used Jimmy as the go-between. One day, a bad toothache or some such thing kept Jimmy away from the set. But even then he was used. The others telephoned him at home to relay messages to the unpopular actor."

Up until a few years ago, Jimmy was in good health. Back in 1970 when he was in London, he underwent an emergency appendicitis operation. "But other than that I feel as strong as the horse I used to ride in my Westerns," he boasted. "Waal, almost."

Recently, he was hospitalized for an irregular heartbeat and for treatment of sciatic nerve pain. "I was advised to give up flying," he said. "I miss it tremendously. On weekends I'd pilot my own Super Piper Cub. But I've lost some of my hearing. And around Los Angeles you'd better be able to hear instructions from the tower or you're in deep trouble. There is a great deal of traffic in the air, and you can't make them repeat instructions."

During a routine examination, doctors discovered that he had developed skin cancer on the left side of his face. It responded to radiation. A hospital spokesperson compared his condition to the minor but recurring skin cancer of Nancy Reagan. "It's rarely fatal," he said.

Jimmy was quickly mobile. He attended a festive ceremony in Washington, D.C. Along with director Elia Kazan, singer Frank Sinatra, ballet dancer-choreographer Katherine Dunham

120

and composer Virgil Thompson, he was the recipient of an award from the Kennedy Center: "For a magnificent contribution to the performing arts." Winners are selected by a committee of outstanding writers and performers. Stewart was selected by Walter Cronkite, Elizabeth Taylor, Ed Asner, Pinchas Zukerman, Edward Albee, Mary Martin, Liv Ullman and other distinguished artists. When the audience rose to applaud, Nancy Reagan, who was seated next to him, leaned over and hugged her husband's old friend.

She and the President invited the Stewarts to a black-tie New Year's Eve party. As usual, Jimmy was the lure. The wife of a prominent cabinet member wanted his autograph. He blushed and stammered, "Are you sure you want mine with all these really important people here?" When she insisted, he told her about a story that had appeared in one of the newspapers.

"They asked if anyone knew who Jimmy Stewart was," he said. "The replies were staggering: 'Could you mean James I of England? But then he was a Stuart!'; 'I know a James F. Stewart who is a typesetter and a member in good standing of the Fraternal Order of Moose Local No. 295!'; 'Or do you have in mind Stewart Granger?'"

Jimmy has been given dozens of honors and awards. Next to the citations he received from the Air Force, he cherishes most his appointment to Princeton University's Board of Trustees. "That honor made his father real happy," said an Indiana, Pennsylvania, neighbor. "When Jimmy was asked to serve, Alex said to me, 'Maybe this acting business isn't so bad after all? I suppose there's still hope for my son. Thank God, he's never gone real Hollywood!'"

Jimmy never has. "I guess I'm sort of one of the less flamboyant actors," he said. "I look at a fellow like Frank Sinatra. I like and admire Frank. But his life-style is not my life-style."

"My husband is much too normal to be an actor," said Gloria. "He shuns nightclubs and likes nothing better than to spend an evening at home."

Henry Fonda once described the Stewart's Tudor-style house:

"as comfortable as Jimmy, with a splash of style thrown in by Gloria." The Stewarts have lived in the same place all of their married life. Located on a good but not gaudy Beverly Hills street, it's very reminiscent of the one the actor grew up in.

When the house next door went on sale, the Stewarts quickly bought it. They promptly tore the adjacent building down and started growing produce in what is probably the most expensive vegetable garden in all of California. "Gloria just planted corn," Jimmy said. "You know, you can grow vegetables in the winter out here. But for some reason, string beans are hard to grow in Beverly Hills. It has something to do with the soil, I think."

"Don't get the impression that Jimmy is minus all faults," his wife said. "At times, it's uphill work to get a word out of him. I can talk myself blue, and his thoughts are way out in left field. As for his being absentminded—well, he does try. He even writes reminders to himself on slips of paper and forgets to look at the slips, or he'll say, 'I've got to be home at four o'clock,' but it escapes his mind."

Stewart often forgets to carry any money with him. Leland Hayward used to tell a story about it: "One day in New York, we had to take a lot of taxis. Naturally, I paid. We went to a restaurant, I paid. It was the same with the hatcheck girl. He borrowed some money to make some telephone calls. I finally blew my top when I had to dig into my pocket to buy him a newspaper. 'Don't you every carry any money?' I yelled.

"I could see that I had really upset him. He looked real unhappy and reached into his pocket. Out came a dried-up, shriveled banana. I burst out laughing. The next day he sent me a gift—a hand-tooled leather wallet that obviously had cost him twenty times the money I'd spent. How could anyone possibly be angry with such a guy?"

Despite these shortcomings, Jimmy was given the Film Institute's Life Achievement Award in 1980. Speaker after speaker lauded his long list of accomplishments. Dustin Hoffman told the audience that his father had worked on the Columbia lot when Stewart was making pictures with Frank Capra. Everybody rose when he turned to Jimmy and said, "I don't think you will be duplicated, although mimicked." They applauded wildly when he added, "After an intensive viewing of your movies, you made me wish for a country we haven't seen for a long while.

"Jimmy Stewart, you made my parents happy. You've made me happy. I'm making sure you make my children happy. And if this world has any kind of luck, you're going to make my grandchildren happy!"

In May of 1984, Jimmy and Gloria attended a Washington, D.C., convention of the World Wildlife Fund-International. Embassy Row was crawling with celebrities as the meeting coincided with a White House state dinner for Mexican President Miguel de la Madrid. Among the VIPs were actor Rock Hudson, billionaire shipping operator George Livanos, Princess Yasmin Aga Khan.

Jimmy, however, drew the most attention. Great Britain's Prince Philip, president of the Wildlife Fund, seemed to express the guests' thoughts when he said, "Thank you for being Jimmy Stewart."

## CHAPTER XVII

# WHY IS JIMMY SO WELL LIKED?

Some years ago, a sociology professor at UCLA asked his students to describe persons they admired and in whom they had confidence. Stewart's name appeared on many of the lists. The responses were revealing:

"Nobody is perfect; probably not even Jimmy Stewart. But he makes you want to believe that people can be honorable, since he is that way."

"He comes off honest, simple, tender-tough. Competent in all cases, yet human. The way we'd all like to be."

"Even the wrong things he does in his pictures turn out to be right. Long before the movie's hour and fifty minutes are up, I wistfully put myself in his boots."

"His personality is like the old, weather-beaten sign on the 3-R Ranch: 'Welcome stranger. If you're peaceable, we'll take care of you. If you ain't, we'll take care of you also.' "

"If another actor spoke his lines, I'd say it was the result of careful rehearsing. In Jimmy's case, I'm convinced he just thought them up."

Estelle Fennell may be the nation's number-one Jimmy Stewart fan. "I've seen every movie he made at least twice," she boasted. "Many of them a lot, lot more. For instance, *The Philadelphia Story*, twenty-three times; *Mr. Smith Goes to Washington*, seventeen times; *The Man Who Shot Liberty Valance*, thirteen times. I know the count exactly, because each time I'd make an entry in my Jimmy Stewart scrapbook. I've filled nine of them with pictures and stories about him."

Such devotion is awesome. However, it isn't unique. Back in the forties and fifties, there were dozens of Jimmy Stewart fan clubs in every state—Pennsylvania led the list with seventy-two of them. Columnist Walter Winchell once told his readers: "Nobody is more dedicated than a Jimmy Stewart buff. I just heard of one lass who hitchhiked 3000 miles to catch a peek of him. On the way she wore out seven pairs of soles. 'My psyche made me,' she sighed. 'But it was worth it.' "

"I didn't have to travel so far," Mrs. Fennell said. "At the time I lived near Hollywood. I became a fan in high school. It continued when I went to work for the telephone company and went on when I got married. My husband used to kid me about the way I idolized Jimmy. Said that I had some kind of sexual complex about him. Maybe there was some truth in that, but I honestly believe it was a whole lot more.

"It's hard to put in words. But maybe this will give you some idea of what I mean. Once Jimmy made a special appearance in a local theater. I was there. The crowd was so thick, his suit jacket got ripped. Somehow, I managed to force my way into the office he'd gone into. Usually, I'm not that forward, but this time I shoved. I always carry a needle and thread in my pocketbook, and when I offered to patch up the rips, he let me. He kept thanking me as if I was the star and he the fan. He was so down to earth. I felt I knew him better than my own family.

"I asked him for an autographed picture. He sent me one. It says, 'To Estelle with loads of good luck for the future.' Well, I wish him exactly the same thing. I hope that his future will be a long one. He deserves it. He has given me a lot of pleasure. God is usually on Jimmy's side."

125

To be continually described that way, the lanky, stammering actor might be a tedious bore. James Maitland Stewart is not. When he was filming *The Stratton Story*, Bill Dickey, the slugging Yankee catcher, was hired to bat against him. "After tossing a dozen wild pitches that usually wound up in the dugout," the celebrated baseball player recalled, "Jimmy managed to toss a very weak one over the plate. I slammed it into the bleachers for a home run. After I circled the bases, the cameras stopped rolling.

"Jimmy temporarily forgot that he was supposed to have an artificial leg and trotted up to me. I've never seen a more cheerful person—you'd think he had just struck out Babe Ruth? 'Now watch my steam,' he said. 'Next stop, the Beverly Hills Kindergarten Team!'

"I thought then and I do now, there goes a high-grade, decent human being."

# A JIMMY STEWART FILMOGRAPHY

The Glenn Miller Story was one of Stewart's most profitable percentage deals. Here, as Glenn Miller, he jams with an all-star jazz ensemble led by Louis Armstrong.

In Alfred Hitchcock's *Rear Window* Stewart played a globe-trotting news photographer confined to a wheelchair with a broken leg. His fiancée, played by Grace Kelly, accuses him of being a Peeping Tom.

Jimmy made four movies with Hitchcock. In *The Man Who Knew Too Much* he played a naive American tourist who accidentally overhears plans for an international murder.

Jimmy had long wanted to film the life story of Charles A. Lindbergh. In 1957 *The Spirit of St. Louis* was finally made, but critics felt the portrayal of the twenty-five-year-old flyer by the forty-seven-year-old actor wasn't credible.

Stewart appeared opposite some of the screen's loveliest actresses. In *Bell, Book and Candle* his leading lady was Kim Novak.

John Wayne and Jimmy were intimate friends. When they appeared in *The Man Who Shot Liberty Valance*, a cameraman said, "I'll bet Damon and Pythias never spent as much time together."

A Father's Day photo of Jimmy with his family in 1956. Rear, left to right: Michael (10), Gloria, Jimmy, Ronald (12). Front, left to right: twin daughters Kelly and Judy (5). (AP/Wide World Photos)

Jimmy was made a brigadier general in the Air Force Reserve. (Courtesy *The Indiana* [Pa.] *Gazette*)

The lanky, sputtering actor frequently demonstrated his marvelous comic talent. A reviewer called Stewart's portrayal of the harassed father in *Mr. Hobbs Takes a Vacation,* "dignified hilarity."

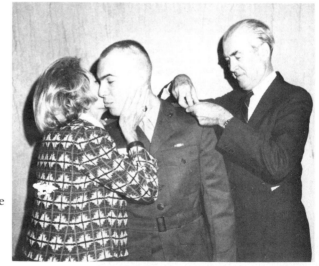

A proud mother and stepfather witnessed their son, Ronald, become a Marine second lieutenant. A short time later the young officer was killed in Vietnam while leading a patrol.
(AP/Wide World Photos)

Jimmy was elated whenever he was given the opportunity to play his accordion in a film. "I always have it handy," he says. "Just in case."

Henry Fonda and Jimmy Stewart admire a group of beautiful girls, among them Shirley Jones, who display their charms in the comedy western, *The Cheyenne Social Club.*

For a good part of his adult life, Jimmy has served on the Los Angeles executive board of the Boy Scouts of America. "Kids are just wonderful," he says.

Stewart won the
Golden Globe Award
for Best Actor in a
Dramatic Series in 1974
for his portrayal of
Billy Jim Hawkins, an
elderly criminal attor-
ney. *The New York Times*
raved that *Hawkins* was
"the most impressively
acted of the new televi-
sion series."

Jimmy and Ronald
Reagan have been close
friends for years.
The President claims
that Stewart was partly
responsible for his
entering politics. Here,
Jimmy helps the politi-
cian campaign in 1976.
(AP/Wide World Photos)

In 1983 Stewart appeared with Bette Davis in a made-for-television movie, *Right of Way.* The outspoken actress said, "There are four remaining superstars: myself, Cagney, Hepburn and Jimmy." About Stewart she added, "And he's the nicest."

Over the years, Jimmy has received numerous awards. One that he particularly treasures was recently given him by the Kennedy Center in Washington, "for a magnificent contribution to the performing arts." From left to right: composer Virgil Thompson, director Elia Kazan, singer Frank Sinatra, dancer Katherine Dunham and Stewart. (AP/ Wide World Photos)

# THE MURDER MAN (MGM—1935)

*Director:* Tim Whelan
*Producer:* Henry Rapf
*Cast:* Spencer Tracy, Virginia Bruce, Lionel Atwill, Harvey Stephens, Robert Barrat, William Collier, Sr., Bobby Watson, William Demarest, James Stewart, Lucien Littlefield, John Sheehan, George Chandler, Fuzzy Knight, Louise Henry, Robert Warrick, Joe Irving, Francis X. Bushman, Jr.
*Authors:* Tim Whelan, Guy Bolton
*Screenplay:* Tim Whelan, John Higgins
*Music:* William Axt
*Editor:* James Newcomb
*Camera:* Lester White
*Art directors:* Cedric Gibbons, Ed Imazu, Edwin Willis
*Sound:* Douglas Shearer
*Running time:* 70 minutes

## ROSE MARIE (MGM—1936)

*Director:* W. S. Van Dyke
*Producer:* Hunt Stromberg
*Cast:* Jeanette MacDonald, Nelson Eddy, Reginald Owen, Allan Jones, Alan
Mowbray, James Stewart, Gilda Gray, George Regas, Robert Greig, Una
O'Connor, Lucien Littlefield, David Niven, Herman Bing, James Mason
*Authors:* Otto Harbach, Oscar Hammerstein II, Rudolf Friml, Herbert
Stothart
*Screenplay:* Frances Goodrich, Albert Hackett, Alice Duer Miller
*Music:* Rudolf Friml, Herbert Stothart, Gus Kahn
*Editor:* Blanche Sewell
*Camera:* William Daniels
*Art directors:* Cedric Gibbons, Joseph Wright, Edwin Willis
*Costumes:* Adrian
*Sound:* Douglas Shearer
*Running time:* 111 minutes

## NEXT TIME WE LOVE (Universal—1936)

*Director:* Edward Griffith
*Producer:* Paul Kohner
*Cast:* Margaret Sullavan, James Stewart, Raymond Milland, Anita Deme-
trio, Grant Mitchell, Robert McWade, Harry Bradley, Jack Daley, Brod-
erick O'Farrell, Hattie McDaniel
*Author:* Ursula Parrott
*Screenplay:* Melville Baker
*Editor:* Ted Kent
*Camera:* Joseph Valentine
*Running time:* 87 minutes

## *WIFE VS. SECRETARY (MGM—1936)*

*Director:* Clarence Brown
*Producer:* Hunt Stromberg
*Cast:* Clark Gable, Jean Harlow, Myrna Loy, May Robson, George Barbier, James Stewart, Hobart Cavanaugh, Tom Dugan, Gilbert Emery, Jack Mulhall, Aileen Pringle
*Author:* Faith Baldwin
*Screenplay:* Norman Krasna, Alice Duer Miller, John Lee Mahin
*Music:* Herbert Stothart, Edward Ward
*Editor:* Frank Hull
*Camera:* Ray June
*Art director:* Cedric Gibbons
*Costumes:* Adrian
*Running time:* 87 minutes

## *SMALL TOWN GIRL (MGM—1936)*

*Director:* William A. Wellman
*Producer:* Hunt Stromberg
*Cast:* Janet Gaynor, Robert Taylor, Binnie Barnes, James Stewart, Lewis Stone, Andy Devine, Elizabeth Patterson, Frank Craven, Douglas Frowley, Isabel Jewell, Charley Grapewin, Edgar Kennedy, William Fung, Thelma Ryan (Mrs. Richard Nixon)
*Author:* Ben Ames Williams
*Screenplay:* John Lee Mahin, Edith Fitzgerald
*Editor:* Blanche Sewell
*Camera:* Charles Rosher
*Art director:* Cedric Gibbons
*Running time:* 90 minutes

## *SPEED (MGM—1936)*

*Director:* Edwin Marin
*Producer:* Lucien Hubbard
*Cast:* James Stewart, Una Merkel, Ted Healy, Wendy Barrie, Weldon Heyburn, Ralph Morgan, Patricia Wilder, Robert Livingston, Walter Kingsford, Jack Clifford
*Authors:* Milton Krims, Larry Bachman
*Screenplay:* Michael Fessier
*Editor:* Harry Poppe
*Camera:* Lester White
*Running time:* 66 minutes

## *THE GORGEOUS HUSSY (MGM—1936)*

*Director:* Clarence Brown
*Producer:* Joseph Mankiewicz
*Cast:* Joan Crawford, Robert Taylor, Lionel Barrymore, Melvyn Douglas, James Stewart, Franchot Tone, Alison Skipworth, Louis Calhern, Melville Cooper, Beulah Bondi, Edith Atwater, Sidney Toler, Gene Lockhart, Phoebe Foster, Louise Beavers, Clara Blandick, Frank Conroy, Nydia Westman, Willard Robertson, Charles Trowbridge, Greta Meyer, Ward Bond
*Author:* Samuel Hopkins Adams
*Screenplay:* Ainsworth Morgan, Stephen Morehouse Avery
*Music:* Herbert Stothart
*Choreography:* Val Raset
*Editor:* Blanche Sewell
*Camera:* George Folsey
*Art director:* Cedric Gibbons
*Running time:* 102 minutes

132

## *BORN TO DANCE (MGM—1936)*

*Director:* Roy Del Ruth
*Producer:* Jack Cummings
*Cast:* Eleanor Powell, James Stewart, Virginia Bruce, Una Merkel, Sid
  Silvers, Frances Langford, Raymond Walburn, Alan Dinehart, Buddy
  Ebsen, Roberta Laurence, William Mandel, Joe Mandel, Juanita Quigley,
  Reginald Gardiner, Dennis O'Keefe, Fuzzy Knight
*Authors:* Jack McGowan, Sid Silvers, B. G. DeSylva
*Screenplay:* Jack McGowan, Sid Silvers
*Music:* Cole Porter
*Musical director:* Alfred Newman
*Musical arrangement:* Roger Edens
*Choreography:* Dave Gould
*Editor:* Blanche Sewell
*Camera:* Ray June
*Running time:* 108 minutes

## *AFTER THE THIN MAN (MGM—1936)*

*Director:* W. S. Van Dyke
*Producer:* Hunt Stromberg
*Cast:* Myrna Loy, William Powell, James Stewart, Joseph Calleia, Elissa
  Landi, Jessie Ralph, Alan Marshall, Sam Levene, Penny Singleton, Wil-
  liam Law, George Zucco, Joe Phillips
*Author:* Dashiell Hammett
*Screenplay:* Frances Goodrich, Albert Hackett
*Music:* Herbert Stothart
*Editor:* Robert Kern
*Camera:* Oliver Marsh
*Sound:* Douglas Shearer
*Running time:* 108 minutes

## SEVENTH HEAVEN (20th Century-Fox— 1937)

*Director:* Henry King
*Producer:* Raymond Griffith
*Cast:* Simone Simon, James Stewart, Gale Sondergaard, Jean Hersholt, Gregory Ratoff, J. Edward Bromberg, John Qualen, Victor Kilian, Thomas Beck, Sig Rumann, Rollo Lloyd, Raffaela Ottiano, Mady Christians, Georges Revavent, Irving Bacon
*Author:* Austin Strong
*Screenplay:* Melville Baker
*Music:* Louis Silvers
*Editor:* Barbara McLean
*Camera:* Merritt Gerstad
*Art director:* William Darling
*Running time:* 100 minutes


## THE LAST GANGSTER (MGM—1937)

*Director:* Edward Ludwig
*Cast:* Edward G. Robinson, James Stewart, Rose Stradner, Lionel Stander, Douglas Scott, John Carradine, Sidney Blackmer, Edward S. Brophy, Alan Baxter, Frank Conroy, Louise Beavers, Grant Mitchell, Horace McMahon, Edward Pawley
*Authors:* William A. Wellman, Robert Carson
*Screenplay:* John Lee Mahin
*Editor:* Ben Lewis
*Camera:* William Daniels
*Art directors:* Cedric Gibbons, Daniel Cathcart, Edwin Willis
*Running time:* 81 minutes

# NAVY BLUE AND GOLD (MGM—1937)

*Director:* Sam Wood
*Producer:* Sam Zimbalist
*Cast:* Robert Young, James Stewart, Lionel Barrymore, Billie Burke, Florence Rice, Tom Brown, Samuel S. Hinds, Paul Kelly, Frank Albertson, Blanche Parker, Minor Watson, Pat Flaherty, Robert Middlemass, Philip Terry, Charles Waldron, Stanley Morner (Dennis Morgan)
*Author:* George Bruce
*Screenplay:* George Bruce
*Music:* Edward Ward
*Editor:* Robert Kern
*Camera:* John Seitz
*Art director:* Cedric Gibbons
*Running time:* 95 minutes

## *OF HUMAN HEARTS (MGM—1938)*

*Director:* Clarence Brown
*Producer:* John W. Considine, Jr.
*Cast:* Walter Huston, James Stewart, Beulah Bondi, Gene Reynolds, Guy
  Kibbee, Charles Coburn, John Carradine, Ann Rutherford, Charley
  Grapewin, Leona Roberts, Max Langston, Gene Lockhart, Leatrice Joy
  Gilbert, Clem Bevans, Sterling Holloway, Charles Peck, Robert
  McWade, Minor Watson, Ward Bond, Philip Terry, Joe Forte
*Author:* Honroé Morrow
*Screenplay:* Bradbury Foote
*Editor:* Frank Hull
*Camera:* Clyde De Vinna
*Art director:* Cedric Gibbons
*Running time:* 100 minutes

## *VIVACIOUS LADY (RKO—1938)*

*Director:* George Stevens
*Producer:* George Stevens
*Cast:* Ginger Rogers, James Stewart, James Ellison, Beulah Bondi, Charles
  Coburn, Frances Mercer, Phyllis Kennedy, Franklin Pangborn, Grady
  Sutton, Jack Carson, Hattie McDaniel
*Author:* I. A. R. Wylie
*Screenplay:* P. I. Wolfson, Ernest Pagano
*Music:* Roy Webb
*Editor:* Henry Berman
*Camera:* Robert de Grasse
*Art directors:* Van Nest Polglase, Carroll Clark, Darrell Silvera
*Costumes:* Irene and Bernard Newman
*Sound:* Hugh McDowell, Jr.
*Running time:* 92 minutes

# THE SHOPWORN ANGEL (MGM—1938)

**Director:** H. C. Potter
**Producer:** Joseph Mankiewicz
**Cast:** Margaret Sullavan, James Stewart, Walter Pidgeon, Nat Pendleton, Sam Levene, Alan Curtis, Hattie McDaniel, Charley Grapewin, Eleanor Lynn, Charles Brown, William Stack, Virginia Gray
**Author:** Dana Burnett
**Screenplay:** Waldo Salt
**Music:** Edward Ward, George Asaf, Felix Powell
**Choreography:** Val Raset
**Editor:** W. Donn Hayes
**Camera:** Joseph Ruttenberg
**Costumes:** Adrian
**Sound:** Douglas Shearer
**Montages:** Slavko Vorkapich
**Running time:** 88 minutes

# YOU CAN'T TAKE IT WITH YOU
## (Columbia—1938)

**Director:** Frank Capra
**Producer:** Frank Capra
**Cast:** Jean Arthur, Lionel Barrymore, James Stewart, Edward Arnold, Mischa Auer, Ann Miller, Spring Byington, Samuel S. Hinds, Donald Meek, H. B. Warner, Halliwell Hobbes, Dub Taylor, Mary Forbes, Lillian Yarbo, Eddie Anderson, Harry Davenport, Clarence Wilson, Charles Lane, Joseph Swickard, Irving Bacon, Ward Bond
**Authors:** George S. Kaufman, Moss Hart
**Screenplay:** Robert Riskin
**Music:** Dmitri Tiomkin
**Music director:** Morris Stoloff
**Editor:** Gene Havlick
**Camera:** Joseph Walker
**Art director:** Stephen Goosson
**Running time:** 125 minutes

# MADE FOR EACH OTHER
## (United Artists— 1939)

*Director:* John Cromwell
*Producer:* David O. Selznick
*Cast:* Carole Lombard, James Stewart, Charles Coburn, Lucile Watson, Harry Davenport, Ruth Weston, Donald Briggs, Eddie Quillan, Louise Beavers, Alma Kruger, Esther Dale, Renee Orsell, Ward Bond, Jack Mulhall, Gary Owen, Jackie Taylor
*Screenplay:* Jo Swerling
*Music director:* Lou Forbes
*Editors:* James Newcomb, Hal Kern
*Camera:* Leon Shamroy, Jack Cosgrove
*Art director:* Lyle Wheeler
*Costumes:* Travis Banton
*Running time:* 90 minutes

# ICE FOLLIES OF 1939 (MGM—1939)

*Director:* Reinhold Schunzel
*Producer:* Harry Rapf
*Cast:* Joan Crawford, James Stewart, Lew Ayres, Lewis Stone, Bess Ehrhardt, Lionel Stander, Charles Brown, Truman Bradley, Marie Blake, Eddy Conrad, Oscar Johnson
*Author:* Leonard Praskins
*Screenplay:* Leonard Praskins, Edgar Woolf, Florence Ryerson
*Music:* Roger Edens
*Editor:* W. Donn Hayes
*Camera:* Joseph Ruttenberg, Oliver Marsh
*Costumes:* Adrian
*Running time:* 85 minutes

## IT'S A WONDERFUL WORLD
## (MGM—1939)

*Director:* W. S. Van Dyke
*Producer:* Frank Davis
*Cast:* Claudette Colbert, James Stewart, Guy Kibbee, Nat Pendleton, Frances Drake, Edgar Kennedy, Ernest Truex, Richard Carle, Cecilia Callejo, Sidney Blackmer, Andy Clyde, Cliff Clark, Cecil Cunningham, Leonard Kilbrick, Grady Sutton, Hans Conried
*Author:* Ben Hecht, Herman Mankiewicz
*Screenplay:* Ben Hecht
*Editor:* Harold Kress
*Camera:* Oliver Marsh
*Art director:* Cedric Gibbons
*Running time:* 86 minutes

## MR. SMITH GOES TO WASHINGTON
## (Columbia—1939)

*Director:* Frank Capra
*Producer:* Frank Capra
*Cast:* Jean Arthur, James Stewart (Academy Award nomination for Best Actor), Claude Rains, Edward Arnold, Guy Kibbee, Thomas Mitchell, Harry Carey, Eugene Pallette, Beulah Bondi, H. B. Warner, Ruth Donnelly, Astrid Allwyn, Grant Mitchell, Richard Grey, Porter Hall, Pierre Watkin, William Demarest, Charles Lane, John Russell, Delmar Watson, Billy Watson, Gary Watson, Larry Sims, H. V. Kaltenborn
*Author:* Lewis Foster
*Screenplay:* Sidney Buchman
*Music:* Dmitri Tiomkin
*Music director:* Morris Stoloff
*Editors:* Gene Havlick, Al Clark
*Camera:* Joseph Walker
*Art director:* Lionel Banks
*Sound:* Slavko Vorkapich
*Running time:* 124 minutes

## DESTRY RIDES AGAIN (Universal—1939)

*Director:* George Marshall
*Producer:* Joseph Pasternak
*Cast:* Marlene Dietrich, James Stewart, Mischa Auer, Charles Winninger, Brian Donlevy, Allen Jenkins, Warren Hymer, Irene Hervey, Una Merkel, Samuel S. Hinds, Lillian Yarbo, Tom Fadden, Billy Gilbert, Ann Todd, Dickie Jones, Chief John Big Tree, Jack Carson, Bill Cody, Jr.
*Author:* Max Brand
*Screenplay:* Felix Jackson, Gertrude Purcell, Henry Myers
*Music:* Frank Skinner, Fredrick Hollander, Frank Loesser
*Music director:* Charles Previn
*Editor:* Milton Carruth
*Camera:* Hal Mohr
*Art director:* Jack Otterson
*Costumes:* Vera West
*Sound:* Bernard Brown
*Running time:* 94 minutes

# THE SHOP AROUND THE CORNER
## (MGM—1940)

*Director:* Ernst Lubitsch
*Producer:* Ernst Lubitsch
*Cast:* Margaret Sullavan, James Stewart, Frank Morgan, Joseph Schild-
kraut, Felix Bressart, Sara Haden, William Tracy, Inez Courtney, Charles
Halton, Edwin Maxwell, Charles Smith, Charles Arnt
*Author:* Nikolaus Laszlo
*Screenplay:* Samson Raphaelson
*Music:* Werner Heymann
*Editor:* George Ruggiero
*Camera:* William Daniels
*Art directors:* Cedric Gibbons, Edwin Willis, Wade Rubottom
*Running time:* 98 minutes

# THE MORTAL STORM (MGM—1940)

*Director:* Frank Borzage
*Cast:* Margaret Sullavan, James Stewart, Robert Young, Frank Morgan,
Irene Rich, William Orr, Robert Stack, Bonita Granville, Maria Ouspen-
skaya, Gene Reynolds, Russell Hicks, William Edmunds, Esther Dale,
Dan Dailey, Jr., Granville Bates, Thomas Ross, Ward Bond, Sue Moore
*Author:* Phyllis Bottome
*Screenplay:* Claudine West, Andersen Ellis, George Froeschel
*Music:* Edward Kane
*Editor:* Elmo Vernon
*Camera:* William Daniels
*Art director:* Cedric Gibbons
*Costumes:* Adrian, Giles Steele
*Sound:* Douglas Shearer
*Makeup:* Jack Dawn
*Running time:* 100 minutes

141

# NO TIME FOR COMEDY (Warner Brothers— 1940)

*Director:* William Keighley
*Producers:* Jack Warner, Hal B. Wallis
*Cast:* James Stewart, Rosalind Russell, Charles Ruggles, Genevieve Tobin,
   Louise Beavers, Allyn Joslyn, Clarence Kolb, Robert Emmett O'Connor,
   Frank Faylen, Edgar Dearing, Robert Greig
*Author:* S. N. Behrman
*Screenplay:* Julius Epstein, Philip Epstein
*Editor:* Owen Marks
*Camera:* Ernest Haller
*Running time:* 93 minutes

# THE PHILADELPHIA STORY (MGM— 1940)

*Director:* George Cukor
*Producer:* Joseph Mankiewicz
*Cast:* Cary Grant, Katharine Hepburn, James Stewart (Academy Award
   winner for Best Actor), Ruth Hussey, Roland Young, John Howard, Vir-
   ginia Weidler, John Halliday, Mary Nash, Henry Daniell, Rex Evans,
   Lionel Pape, Russ Clark, Hilda Plowright, Hillary Brooke
*Author:* Philip Barry
*Screenplay:* Donald Ogden Stewart
*Music:* Franz Waxman
*Editor:* Frank Sullivan
*Camera:* Joseph Ruttenberg
*Art directors:* Cedric Gibbons, Wade Rubottom, Edwin Willis
*Costumes:* Adrian
*Sound:* Douglas Shearer
*Makeup:* Jack Dawn
*Running time:* 112 minutes

## COME LIVE WITH ME (MGM—1941)

**Director:** Clarence Brown
**Producer:** Clarence Brown
**Cast:** James Stewart, Hedy Lamarr, Ian Hunter, Donald Meek, Verree
  Teasdale, Barton MacLane, Edward Ashley, Ann Codee, King Baggot,
  Adeline de Walt Reynolds, Frank Orth, Frank Faylen, Horace
  McMahon, Greta Meyer, Si Jenks, Dewey Robinson, Joe Yule
**Author:** Virginia Van Upp
**Screenplay:** Patterson McNutt
**Editor:** Frank Hull
**Camera:** George Folsey
**Art director:** Cedric Gibbons
**Running time:** 85 minutes

## POT O' GOLD (United Artists—1941)

**Director:** George Marshall
**Producer:** James Roosevelt
**Cast:** James Stewart, Paulette Goddard, Charles Winninger, Mary Gordon,
  Frank Melton, Jed Prouty, Dick Hogan, James Burke, Charles Arnt,
  Donna Wood, Henry Roquemore, Larry Cotton, Horace Heidt
**Author:** Monte Brice, Andrew Bennison, Harry Tugend
**Screenplay:** Walter de Leon
**Music:** Hy Heath and Fred Rose, Dave Franklin, Lou Forbes and Henry
  Sullivan, Mack David and Vee Lawnhurst
**Editor:** Lloyd Nosler
**Camera:** Hal Mohr
**Running time:** 86 minutes

## *ZIEGFELD GIRL (MGM—1941)*

*Director:* Robert Z. Leonard
*Producer:* Pandro Berman
*Cast:* James Stewart, Judy Garland, Hedy Lamarr, Lana Turner, Tony
  Martin, Jackie Cooper, Ian Hunter, Charles Winninger, Edward Everett
  Horton, Philip Dorn, Paul Kelly, Eve Arden, Dan Dailey, Jr., Al Shean,
  Fay Holden, Felix Bressart, Ed McNamara, Rose Hobart, Mae Busch,
  Joyce Compton, Jean Wallace, Joe Yule, Horace McMahon, Si Jenks
*Author:* William Anthony McGuire
*Screenplay:* Marguerite Roberts, Sonya Levien
*Music:* Herbert Stothart
*Musical numbers:* Busby Berkeley
*Music director:* George Stoll
*Editor:* Blanche Sewell
*Camera:* Ray June
*Art directors:* Cedric Gibbons, Daniel Cathcart
*Set director:* Edwin Willis
*Costumes:* Adrian
*Sound:* Douglas Shearer
*Makeup:* Jack Dawn
*Running time:* 131 minutes

# IT'S A WONDERFUL LIFE (RKO—1946)

**Director:** Frank Capra
**Producer:** Frank Capra
**Cast:** James Stewart (Academy Award nomination for Best Actor), Donna
Reed, Lionel Barrymore, Thomas Mitchell, Henry Travers, Beulah Bondi,
Frank Faylen, Ward Bond, Gloria Grahame, H. B. Warner, Sam Wain-
wright, Samuel S. Hinds, Frank Albertson, Virginia Patton, Bill Edmunds,
Bobby Anderson, Jean Gale, Jeanine Anne Roose, Danny Mummert,
George Nokes, Sheldon Leonard
**Author:** Philip Van Doren
**Screenplay:** Frances Goodrich, Albert Hackett, Joe Swerling, Frank Capra
**Music:** Dmitri Tiomkin
**Editor:** William Hornbeck
**Camera:** Joseph Walker, Joseph Biroc
**Art director:** Jack Okey
**Set director:** Emile Kuri
**Sound:** Richard Van Hessen, Clark Portman
**Running time:** 129 minutes

## MAGIC TOWN (RKO—1947)

**Director:** William A. Wellman
**Producer:** Robert Riskin
**Cast:** James Stewart, Jane Wyman, Kent Smith, Ned Sparks, Wallace Ford, Donald Meek, Regis Toomey, Ann Shoemaker, Howard Freeman, Harry Holman, Mickey Kuhn, Mary Currier, Selmer Jackson, Mickey Roth, Robert Dudley, Frank Darien, Larry Wheat, Jimmy Crane, Griff Barnett
**Author:** Joseph Krumgold
**Screenplay:** Robert Riskin
**Music:** Roy Webb
**Music director:** C. Bakaleinikoff
**Editors:** Richard Wray, Sherman Todd
**Camera:** Joseph Biroc
**Art director:** Lionel Banks
**Running time:** 103 minutes

## CALL NORTHSIDE 777 (20th Century-Fox—1947)

**Director:** Henry Hathaway
**Producer:** Otto Lang
**Cast:** James Stewart, Richard Conte, Lee J. Cobb, Helen Walker, Kasia Orzazewski, Paul Harvey, Howard Smith, George Tyne, Richard Bishop, Percy Helton, Charles Lane, Jane Crawley, Otto Waldis, Michael Chapin, Addison Richards, John Bleifer, Samuel S. Hinds, Lou Eckels, E. G. Marshall, Thelma Ritter, Lionel Stander, J. M. Kerrigan
**Authors:** James McGuire, Leonard Hoffman
**Screenplay:** Jerome Cady, Jay Dratler
**Music:** Alfred Newman, Edward Powell
**Editor:** J. Watson Webb, Jr.
**Camera:** Joe MacDonald
**Art directors:** Lyle Wheeler, Mark Lee Kirk
**Costumes:** Kay Nelson
**Sound:** W. D. Flick, Roger Heyman
**Special effects:** Fred Sersen
**Makeup:** Ben Nye
**Running time:** 111 minutes

## *ON OUR MERRY WAY (United Artists—1948)*

*Directors:* King Vidor, Leslie Fenton
*Producers:* Benedict Bogeaus, Burgess Meredith
*Cast:* Paulette Goddard, James Stewart, Henry Fonda, Burgess Meredith,
    Fred MacMurray, Hugh Herbert, William Demarest, Eduardo Ciannelli,
    Charles Brown, Dorothy Ford, Betty Caldwell, Frank Moran, Carl
    Switzer, David Whorf, Nana Bryant, Harry James
*Authors:* Arch Obler, John O'Hara, Lou Breslow
*Screenplay:* Laurence Stallings
*Music:* Heinz Roemheld, Henry Russell, Skitch Henderson
*Music director:* David Chudnow
*Editor:* James Smith
*Camera:* John Seitz, Ernest Laszlo, Gordon Avil
*Art directors:* Ernst Fegte, Duncan Cramer
*Set directors:* Eugene Redd, Robert Priestly
*Costumes:* Greta
*Sound:* William Lynch
*Makeup:* Otis Malcom
*Running time:* 107 minutes

## *ROPE (Warner Brothers—1948)*

*Director:* Alfred Hitchcock
*Producers:* Sidney Bernstein, Alfred Hitchcock
*Cast:* James Stewart, John Dall, Farley Granger, Cedric Hardwicke, Joan
    Chandler, Constance Collier, Douglas Dick, Edith Evanson, Dick Hogan
*Author:* Patrick Hamilton
*Screenplay:* Arthur Laurents, Hume Cronyn
*Music:* Leo Forbstein
*Editor:* William Ziegler
*Camera:* Joseph Valentine, William Skall
*Art director:* Perry Forbstein
*Costumes:* Adrian
*Running time:* 80 minutes

# *YOU GOTTA STAY HAPPY (Universal—1948)*

*Director:* H. C. Potter
*Executive producer:* William Dozier
*Producer:* Karl Tunberg
*Cast:* Joan Fontaine, James Stewart, Eddie Albert, Roland Young, Willard Parker, Percy Kilbride, Porter Hall, Marcy McGuire, Arthur Walsh, Halliwell Hobbes, Paul Cavanagh, Mary Forbes, Don Kohler, Edith Evanson, Bert Conway, Emory Parnell, Robert Rockwell, Jimmy Dodd, Edward Gargan
*Author:* Robert Carson
*Screenplay:* Karl Tunberg
*Music:* Daniele Amfitheatrof
*Orchestrator:* David Tamkin
*Music director:* Milton Schwarzwald
*Editor:* Paul Wetherwax
*Camera:* Russell Metty
*Art directors:* Russell Gausman, Ruby Levitt, Alexander Golitzen
*Costumes:* Jean Louis
*Sound:* Leslie Carey, Joseph Lapis
*Special effects:* David Horsley
*Makeup:* Bud Westmore, Leo LaCava
*Running time:* 100 minutes

# THE STRATTON STORY (MGM—1949)

**Director:** Sam Wood
**Producer:** Jack Cummings
**Cast:** James Stewart, June Allyson, Frank Morgan, Agnes Moorehead, Bill
    Williams, Bruce Cowling, Eugene Bearden, Cliff Clark, Mary Lawrence,
    Dean White, Robert Gist, Mervyn Shea, Mitchell Lewis, Michael Ross,
    Lee Tung Foo, Bill Dickey, Jimmy Dykes
**Author:** Douglas Morrow
**Screenplay:** Guy Trosper
**Technical advisor:** Monty Stratton
**Assistant director:** Sid Sidman
**Music:** Adolph Deutsch
**Editor:** Ben Lewis
**Camera:** Harold Rosson
**Art directors:** Cedric Gibbons, Paul Groesse
**Set directors:** Edwin Willis, Ralph Hurst
**Costumes:** Helen Rose
**Makeup:** Jack Dawn
**Sound:** Douglas Shearer, Charles Wallace
**Special effects:** Arnold Gillespie
**Montages:** Peter Ballbusch
**Running time:** 106 minutes

## *MALAYA (MGM—1949)*

*Director:* Richard Thorpe
*Producer:* Edwin Knopf
*Cast:* Spencer Tracy, James Stewart, Valentina Cortese, Sydney Green-
    street, John Hodiak, Lionel Barrymore, Gilbert Roland, Richard Loo,
    Roland Winters, Lester Mathews, Ian MacDonald, Paul Kruger, Tom
    Helmore, Herbert Heywood
*Author:* Manchester Boddy
*Screenplay:* Frank Fenton
*Assistant director:* Bert Glazer
*Music:* Bronislau Kaper
*Musical director:* Andre Previn
*Editor:* Ben Lewis
*Camera:* George Folsey
*Art directors:* Cedric Gibbons, Malcolm Brown
*Set directors:* Edwin Willis, Henry Grace
*Costumes:* Irene
*Sound:* Douglas Shearer
*Special effects:* Arnold Gillespie, Warren Newcombe
*Running time:* 98 minutes

# WINCHESTER '73 *(Universal—1950)*

*Director:* Anthony Mann
*Producer:* Aaron Rosenberg
*Cast:* James Stewart, Shelley Winters, Dan Duryea, Stephen McNally, Millard Mitchell, Charles Drake, John McIntire, Will Geer, Jay C. Flippen, Rock Hudson, John Alexander, James Millican, Abner Biberman, James Best, Carol Henry, Tony Curtis
*Author:* Stuart N. Lake
*Screenplay:* Robert Richards, Borden Chase
*Music director:* Joseph Gershenson
*Editor:* Edward Curtiss
*Camera:* William Daniels
*Art directors:* Bernard Herzbrun, Nathan Juran
*Costumes:* Jean Louis
*Makeup:* Bud Westmore
*Running time:* 93 minutes

# BROKEN ARROW *(20th Century-Fox—1950)*

*Director:* Delmer Daves
*Producer:* Julian Blaustein
*Cast:* James Stewart, Jeff Chandler, Debra Paget, Basil Ruysdael, Will Geer, Joyce Mackenzie, Arthur Hunnicutt, Raymond Bramley, Jay Silverheels, Argentina Brunetti, Robert Dover, Jack Lee, Mickey Kuhn, Robert Adler, Chris Willow Bird, John War Eagle, Iron Eyes Cody
*Music director:* Alfred Newman
*Editor:* Watson Webb, Jr.
*Camera:* Ernest Palmer
*Art directors:* Lyle Wheeler, Arthur Hogsett
*Costumes:* Kay Nelson
*Sound:* W. D. Flick
*Running time:* 93 minutes

## THE JACKPOT (20th Century-Fox— 1950)

*Director:* Walter Lang
*Producer:* Samuel Engel
*Cast:* James Stewart, Barbara Hale, James Gleason, Fred Clark, Alan Mowbray, Patricia Medina, Natalie Wood, Tommy Rettig, Lyle Talbot, Charles Tannen, Bigelow Sayre, Dick Cogan, Jewel Rose, Eddie Firestone, Estelle Etterre, Caryl Lincoln, Valerie Mark, Joan Miller, Walter Baldwin, Kim Spalding, Ann Doran, Sam Edwards
*Author:* John McNulty
*Screenplay:* Phoebe and Henry Ephron
*Music:* Earle Hagen
*Editor:* Watson Webb, Jr.
*Camera:* Joseph La Shelle
*Art directors:* Lyle Wheeler, Joseph Wright
*Running time:* 85 minutes

## HARVEY (Universal— 1950)

*Director:* Henry Koster
*Producer:* John Beck
*Cast:* James Stewart (Academy Award nomination for Best Actor), Josephine Hull, Peggy Dow, Charles Drake, Cecil Kellaway, Victoria Horne, Jesse White, William Lynn, Wallace Ford, Nana Bryant, Grace Mills, Clem Bevans, Ida Moore, Richard Wessel, Ed Max, Anna O'Neal, Polly Bailey, Minerva Urecal
*Author:* Mary Chase
*Screenplay:* Mary Chase, Oscar Brodney
*Music:* Frank Skinner
*Editor:* Ralph Dawson
*Camera:* William Daniels
*Art directors:* Bernard Herzbrun, Nathan Juran
*Makeup:* Bud Westmore
*Running time:* 104 minutes

# NO HIGHWAY IN THE SKY
## *(20th Century-Fox— 1951)*

*Director:* Henry Koster
*Producer:* Louis K. Lighton
*Cast:* James Stewart, Marlene Dietrich, Glynis Johns, Jack Hawkins, Janette Scott, Elizabeth Allan, Ronald Squire, Jill Clifford, Niall MacGinnis, David Hutcheson, Hugh Wakefield, Michael Kingsley, Feliz Aylmer, John Salew, Douglas Bradley Smith, Hugh Gross
*Author:* Nevil Shute
*Screenplay:* R. C. Sherriff, Oscar Millard, Alec Coppel
*Assistant director:* Bluey Hill
*Editor:* Manuel Del Campo
*Camera:* George Perinal
*Art director:* C. P. Norman
*Wardrobe for Marlene Dietrich:* Christian Dior
*Sound:* Buster Ambler
*Running time:* 98 minutes

# THE GREATEST SHOW ON EARTH
## *(Paramount— 1952)*

*Director:* Cecil B. De Mille
*Producer:* Cecil B. De Mille
*Cast:* Betty Hutton, Cornel Wilde, Charlton Heston, Dorothy Lamour,
Gloria Grahame, James Stewart, Henry Wilcoxon, Emmett Kelly, John
Kellogg, Lillian Albertson, Lyle Bettger, Lawrence Tierney, Julia Faye,
Bob Carson, Antoinette Concello, Dorothy Crider, John Ringling North,
Edmond O'Brien, William Boyd, Mona Freeman, Bing Crosby,
Bob Hope
*Author:* Fredric Frank, Frank Cavett
*Screenplay:* Fredric Frank, Barre Lyndon, Theodore St. John
*Assistant director:* Edward Salvern
*Assistant producer:* Henry Wilcoxon
*Editor:* Anne Bauchens
*Camera:* George Barnes, J. Peverell Marley, Wallace Kelley
*Art directors:* Hal Pereira, Walter Tyler
*Set directors:* Sam Comer, Ray Moyer
*Circus costumes:* Miles White
*Wardrobe:* Edith Head, Dorothy Jeakins
*Makeup:* Wally Westmore
*Sound:* Henry Lindgren
*Special effects:* Gordon Jennings, Paul Lerpae
*Circus dance numbers stage by:* John Murray Anderson
*Running time:* 153 minutes

## BEND OF THE RIVER *(Universal—1952)*

*Director:* Anthony Mann
*Producer:* Aaron Rosenberg
*Cast:* James Stewart, Arthur Kennedy, Julia Adams, Rock Hudson, Jay C.
  Flippen, Lori Nelson, Henry Morgan, Jack Lambert, Chubby Johnson,
  Royal Dano, Howard Petrie, Stepin Fetchit, Cliff Lyons, Lillian Ran-
  dolph, Frances Bavier, Frank Ferguson, Gregg Barton
*Screenplay:* Borden Chase
*Music:* Hans J. Salter
*Editor:* Russell Schoengarth
*Art directors:* Bernard Herzbrun, Nathan Juran
*Running time:* 91 minutes

## CARBINE WILLIAMS *(MGM—1952)*

*Director:* Richard Thorpe
*Producer:* Armand Deutsch
*Cast:* James Stewart, Jean Hagen, Paul Stewart, Otto Hulett, Rhys
  Williams, Herbert Hayes, James Arness, Porter Hall, Fay Roope, Leif
  Erickson, Howard Petrie, Frank Richards, Stuart Randall, Dan Ross,
  Bobby Hyatt, Richard Reeves, Duke York, Bert LeBaron, Norma Jean
  Cramer, Sam Flint
*Author:* Art Cohn
*Screenplay:* Art Cohn
*Music:* Conrad Salinger
*Editor:* Newell Kimlin
*Camera:* William Mellor
*Assistant directors:* Cedric Gibbons, Eddie Imazu
*Running time:* 91 minutes

## THE NAKED SPUR (MGM—1953)

*Director:* Anthony Mann
*Producer:* William H. Wright
*Cast:* James Stewart, Janet Leigh, Robert Ryan, Ralph Meeker, Millard Mitchell
*Screenplay:* Sam Rolfe, Harold Jack Bloom
*Music:* Bronislau Kaper
*Editor:* George White
*Camera:* William Mellor
*Art directors:* Cedric Gibbons, Malcolm Brown
*Running time:* 91 minutes

## THUNDER BAY (Universal—1953)

*Director:* Anthony Mann
*Producer:* Aaron Rosenberg
*Cast:* James Stewart, Joanne Dru, Gilbert Roland, Dan Duryea, Jay C. Flippen, Marcia Henderson, Robert Monet, Gladys Miller, Antonio Moreno, Henry Morgan, Fortunio Bonanova, Mario Siletti, Antoine Chighizola
*Authors:* Michael Hayes, George W. George, George F. Slavin
*Screenplay:* Gil Doud, John Michael Hayes
*Editor:* Russell Schoengarth
*Camera:* William Daniels
*Art directors:* Alexander Golitzen, Richard Riedel
*Running time:* 103 minutes

# *THE GLENN MILLER STORY (Universal—1954)*

*Director:* Anthony Mann
*Producer:* Aaron Rosenberg
*Cast:* James Stewart, June Allyson, Charles Drake, George Tobias, Henry Morgan, Frances Langford, Marion Ross, Irving Bacon, Kathleen Lockhart, Barton MacLane, Ruth Hampton, Sig Ruman, Babe Russin, James Bell, Katherine Warren, Iouis Armstrong, Gene Krupa, Phil Harris, Ben Pollack
*Screenplay:* Valentine Davies, Oscar Brodney
*Assistant director:* John Sherwood
*Music:* Henry Mancini
*Musical director:* Joseph Gershenson
*Editor:* Russell Schoengarth
*Camera:* William Daniels
*Art directors:* Bernard Herzbrun, Alexander Golitzen
*Choreography:* Kenny Williams
*Running time:* 116 minutes

## *REAR WINDOW (Paramount—1954)*

**Director:** Alfred Hitchcock
**Producer:** Alfred Hitchcock
**Cast:** James Stewart, Grace Kelly, Wendell Corey, Thelma Ritter, Raymond Burr, Judith Evelyn, Ross Bagdassarian, Georgine Darcy, Sara Berner, Frank Cady, Jesslyn Fax, Rand Harper, Irene Winston, Harris Davenport, Marla English, Kathryn Grant, Alan Lee, Anthony Warde, Bess Flowers, Barbara Bailey
**Author:** Cornell Woolrich
**Screenplay:** John Hayes
**Assistant director:** Herbert Coleman
**Music:** Franz Waxman
**Editor:** George Tomasini
**Camera:** Robert Burks
**Art directors:** Hal Pereira, Joseph M. Johnson
**Set directors:** Sam Gomer, Ray Mayer
**Costumes:** Edith Head
**Sound:** Harry Lindgren
**Special effects:** John P. Fulton
**Running time:** 112 minutes

# *THE FAR COUNTRY (Universal—1955)*

**Director:** Anthony Mann
**Producer:** Aaron Rosenberg
**Cast:** James Stewart, Ruth Roman, Corinne Calvert, Walter Brennan, Jay
  C. Flippen, John McIntire, Henry Morgan, Steve Brodie, Royal Dano,
  Jack Elam, Chubby Johnson, Eddy Waller, Clay Wilkerson, Robert
  Foulk, Eugene Borden, Alan Ray
**Screenplay:** Borden Chase
**Assistant directors:** John Sherwood, Ronnie Rondell, Terry Nelson
**Musical director:** Joseph Gershenson
**Editor:** Russell Schoengarth
**Camera:** William Daniels
**Art directors:** Bernard Hertzbrun, Alexander Golitzen
**Running time:** 96 minutes

# *STRATEGIC AIR COMMAND (Paramount—1955)*

**Director:** Anthony Mann
**Producer:** Samuel Briskin
**Cast:** James Stewart, June Allyson, Frank Lovejoy, Barry Sullivan, Alex
  Nicol, Bruce Bennett, Jay C. Flippen, James Millican, James Bell, Rich-
  ard Shannon, Rosemary DeCamp, John McKee, Glenn Denning, Len
  Hendry, David Vaile, Vernon Rich
**Screenplay:** Valentine Davies, Beirne Lay, Jr.
**Assistant director:** John Coonan
**Musical director:** Victor Young
**Editor:** Eda Warren
**Camera:** William Daniels, Farciot Edouart, John Fulton, Thomas Tutwiler
**Art directors:** Hal Pereira, Earl Hedrick
**Running time:** 114 minutes

159

# THE MAN FROM LARAMIE (Columbia—1955)

**Director:** Anthony Mann
**Producer:** William Goetz
**Cast:** James Stewart, Arthur Kennedy, Donald Crisp, Cathy O'Donnell, Wallace Ford, Jack Elam, John War Eagle, James Millican, Greg Barton, Boyd Stockman, Frank Cordell, Frank del Kova, Jack Carry, Bill Lewis, Frosty Royce, Eddy Waller
**Author:** Thomas T. Flynn
**Screenplay:** Philip Yordan, Frank Burt
**Music:** George Duning
**Editor:** William Lyon
**Camera:** Charles Lang
**Art director:** Cary Odell
**Sound:** George Cooper
**Running time:** 103 minutes

# THE MAN WHO KNEW TOO MUCH
## (Paramount— 1956)

*Director:* Alfred Hitchcock
*Producer:* Alfred Hitchcock
*Associate producer:* Herbert Coleman
*Cast:* James Stewart, Doris Day, Brenda de Banzie, Bernard Miles, Ralph Truman, Daniel Gelin, Mogens Wieth, Alan Mowbray, Hillary Brooke, Christopher Olsen, Reggie Nalder, Richard Wattis, Noel Willman, Alix Talton, Yves Brainville, Carolyn Jones, Betty Baskcomb, Patrick Aherne
*Authors:* Charles Bennett, D. B. Wyndham-Lewis
*Screenplay:* John M. Hayes, Angus MacPhail
*Assistant director:* Howard Joslin
*Music:* Bernard Herrmann
*Editor:* George Tomasini
*Camera:* Robert Burks
*Art director:* Hal Pereira
*Set directors:* Sam Comer, Arthur Kram
*Costumes:* Edith Head
*Sound:* Franz Paul, Gene Garvin
*Special effects:* John Fulton
*Running time:* 120 minutes

# *THE SPIRIT OF ST. LOUIS (Warner Brothers— 1957)*

*Director:* Billy Wilder
*Producer:* Leland Hayward
*Cast:* James Stewart, Murray Hamilton, Patricia Smith, Bartlette Robinson, Robert Cornthwaite, Shelia Bond, Marc Connelly, Arthur Space, Harlan Wade, Dabbs Greer, Paul Birch, David Orrick, Griff Barnett, Syd Saylor, Aaron Spelling
*Author:* Charles A. Lindbergh
*Adaptor:* Charles Lederer
*Screenplay:* Billy Wilder, Wendell Mayes
*Music:* Franz Waxman
*Orchestrator:* Leonid Raab
*Editor:* Arthur P. Schmidt
*Camera:* Robert Burks, J. Peverell Marley
*Art director:* Art Loel
*Set director:* William Kuehl
*Technical advisors:* Major General Victor Bertrandias, U.S.A.F., Harlan Gurney
*Special effects:* H. F. Koenekamp, Louis Lichtenfield
*Montages:* Charles Eames
*Running time:* 135 minutes

# *NIGHT PASSAGE (Universal— 1957)*

*Director:* James Neilson
*Producer:* Aaron Rosenberg
*Cast:* James Stewart, Audie Murphy, Dan Duryea, Dianne Foster, Elaine Stewart, Brandon de Wilde, Jay C. Flippen, Herbert Anderson, Jack Elam, Tommy Cook, Paul Fix, Olive Carey, James Flavin, Donald Curtis, Ellen Corby, Polly Burson
*Author:* Norman A. Fox
*Screenplay:* Borden Chase
*Assistant director:* Marshall Green
*Music:* Dmitri Tiomkin
*Editor:* Sherman Todd
*Camera:* William Daniels, Clifford Stine
*Art directors:* Alexander Golitzen, Robert Clatworthy
*Running time:* 90 minutes

## *VERTIGO (Paramount— 1958)*

*Director:* Alfred Hitchcock
*Producer:* Alfred Hitchcock
*Associate producer:* Herbert Coleman
*Cast:* James Stewart, Kim Novak, Barbara Bel Geddes, Tom Helmore, Henry Jones, Raymond Bailey, Konstantin Shayne, Ellen Corby, Lee Patrick, Paul Bryar, Fred Graham
*Author:* Pierre Boileau, Thomas Narcejac
*Screenplay:* Alec Coppel, Samuel Taylor
*Assistant director:* Daniel McCauley
*Music:* Bernard Herrmann
*Musical director:* Muir Mathieson
*Editor:* George Fulton
*Camera:* Robert Burks
*Art director:* Hal Pereira
*Set directors:* Sam Comer, Frank McKellvey
*Costumes:* Edith Head
*Makeup:* Wally Westmore
*Sound:* Harold Lewis, Winston Leverett
*Special effects:* John Fulton
*Running time:* 121 minutes

## *BELL, BOOK AND CANDLE (Columbia— 1958)*

*Director:* Richard Quine
*Producer:* Julian Blaustein
*Cast:* James Stewart, Kim Novak, Jack Lemmon, Ernie Kovacs, Hermoine Gingold, Elsa Lanchester, Janice Rule, Phillips Clay, Bek Nelson, Howard McNear, Wolf Barzell, Gail Bonney, Monty Ash, Joe Barry, James Lamphier, Sister Little
*Author:* John Van Druten
*Screenplay:* Daniel Taradash
*Music:* George Duning
*Editor:* Charles Nelson
*Camera:* James Wong Howe
*Art director:* Cary Odell
*Set director:* Louis Diage
*Costumes:* Jean Louis
*Sound:* Franklin Hansen, Jr.
*Running time:* 103 minutes

# *ANATOMY OF A MURDER (Columbia—1959)*

*Director:* Otto Preminger
*Producer:* Otto Preminger
*Cast:* James Stewart (Academy Award nomination for Best Actor), Lee
  Remick, Ben Gazzara, Arthur O'Connell, Eve Arden, Kathryn Grant,
  George C. Scott, Joseph N. Welch, Brooks West, Murray Hamilton,
  Orson Bean, Alexander Campbell, Joseph Kearns, Russ Brown, Howard
  McNear, Jimmy Durgo, Duke Ellington
*Author:* Robert Traver
*Screenplay:* Wendell Mayes
*Assistant director:* David Silver
*Music:* Duke Ellington
*Editor:* Louis Loeffler
*Camera:* Sam Leavitt
*Art director:* Boris Leven
*Set director:* Howard Bristol
*Wardrobe:* Michael Harte
*Makeup:* Del Armstrong, Harry Ray
*Sound:* Jack Solomon
*Running time:* 160 minutes

# *THE FBI STORY (Warner Brothers—1959)*

*Director:* Mervyn LeRoy
*Producer:* Mervyn LeRoy
*Cast:* James Stewart, Vera Miles, Murray Hamilton, Nick Adams, Diane
  Jergens, Jean Willes, Victor Millan, Joyce Taylor, Parley Baer, Fay
  Roope, Ed Prentis, Robert Gist, Kenneth Mayer, Paul Genge, Ann
  Doran, Forrest Taylor, Scott Peters, William Phipps
*Author:* Don Whitehead
*Screenplay:* Richard Breen, John Twist
*Assistant directors:* David Silver, Gil Kessel
*Music:* Max Steiner
*Orchestrator:* Philip Anderson
*Camera:* Joseph Biroc
*Art director:* John Beckman
*Set director:* Ralph Hurst
*Costumes:* Adele Palmer
*Makeup:* Gordon Bau
*Sound:* M. A. Merrick
*Running time:* 149 minutes

164

# *THE MOUNTAIN ROAD (Columbia—1960)*

*Director:* Daniel Mann
*Producer:* William Goetz
*Cast:* James Stewart, Lisa Lu, Glenn Corbett, Henry Morgan, Frank Silvera, Mike Kellin, James Best, Rudy Bond, Frank Maxwell, Eddie Firestone, Leo Chen, Alan Baxter, Bill Quinn, Peter Chong, P. C. Lee, Frank Tso Wang
*Author:* Theodore White
*Screenplay:* Alfred Hayes
*Assistant director:* Irving Moore
*Music:* Jerome Moross
*Musical director:* Morris Stoloff
*Editor:* Edward Curtiss
*Camera:* Burnett Guffey
*Art director:* Cary Odell
*Set directors:* Bill Calvert, Sidney Clifford
*Wardrobe:* Michael Harte
*Makeup:* Ben Lane
*Sound:* John Livadary
*Running time:* 103 minutes

# TWO RODE TOGETHER (Columbia—1961)

**Director:** John Ford
**Producer:** Stan Sheptner
**Cast:** James Stewart, Richard Widmark, Shirley Jones, Linda Cristal, Andy
   Devine, John McIntire, Paul Birch, Henry Brandon, Willis Bouchey,
   Harry Carey, Jr., Olive Carey, Mae Marsh, Jeanette Nolan, Ken Curtis,
   Chet Douglas, Annelle Hayes, David Kent, Anna Lee, Ford Rainey,
   Woody Strode, John Qualen, O. Z. Whitehead, Big John Hamilton, Ted
   Knight
**Author:** Will Cook
**Screenplay:** Frank Nugent
**Assistant director:** Wingate Smith
**Music:** George Duning
**Orchestrator:** Arthur Morton
**Editor:** Jack Murray
**Camera:** Charles Lawton, Jr.
**Art director:** Robert Peterson
**Set director:** James M. Crowe
**Makeup:** Ben Lane
**Sound:** Charles J. Rice, Harry Mills
**Running time:** 108 minutes

# X-15 (United Artists—1961)

*Director:* Richard Donner
*Producer:* Henry Sanicola, Tony Lazzarino
*Narrator:* James Stewart
*Cast:* David McLean, Charles Bronson, Ralph Taeger, James Gregory, Brad Dexter, Kenneth Tobey, Mary Tyler Moore, Patricia Owens, Lisabeth Hush, Ethel Moore, Lauren Gilbert, Phil Dean, Chuck Stanford, Patty McDonald, Grant Webster, Mike MacKane, Robert Dornam, Frank Watkins, Barbara Kelley, Darlene Hendricks, Phil Marrott
*Screenplay:* Tony Lazzarino, James Warner Bellah
*Assistant directors:* Russ Haverick, Jay Sandrich
*Music:* Nathan Scott
*Editor:* Stanley Rabjohn
*Camera:* Carl Guthrie
*Art director:* Rolland Brooks
*Set director:* Kenneth Schwartz
*Makeup:* Beans Pondell
*Running time:* 107 minutes

# THE MAN WHO SHOT LIBERTY VALANCE
## (Paramount— 1962)

**Director:** John Ford
**Producer:** Willis Goldbeck
**Cast:** John Wayne, James Stewart, Vera Miles, Lee Marvin, Edmond
O'Brien, Andy Devine, Woody Strode, John Qualen, Ken Murray,
Jeanette Nolan, Strother Martin, Lee Van Cleef, Willis Bouchey, Carleton
Young, Denver Pyle, O. Z. Whitehead, Paul Birch, Joseph Hoover, Larry
Finley, Chuck Roberson
**Author:** Dorothy Johnson
**Screenplay:** James Warner Bellah, Willis Goldbeck
**Assistant director:** Wingate Smith
**Music:** Cyril Mockridge
**Editor:** Otho Lovering
**Camera:** William Clothier
**Art directors:** Hal Pereira, Eddie Imazu
**Makeup:** Wally Westmore
**Sound:** Phil Mitchell
**Running time:** 123 minutes

# MR. HOBBS TAKES A VACATION
## (20th Century-Fox— 1962)

*Director:* Henry Koster
*Producer:* Jerry Wald
*Associate producer:* Marvin Gluck
*Cast:* James Stewart, Maureen O'Hara, Fabian, John Saxon, Marie Wilson, Reginald Gardiner, Laurie Peters, Valerie Varda, John McGiver, Lili Gentle, Natalie Trundy, Michael Burns, Josh Pine, Richard Collier, Peter Oliphant, Thomas Lowell, Stephen Mines, Dennie Whitcomb, Michael Sean, Darryl Duke
*Author:* Edward Streeter
*Screenplay:* Nunnally Johnson
*Assistant director:* Joseph Rickards
*Music:* Henry Mancini
*Orchestrators:* Jack Hays, Leo Shuken
*Editor:* Marjorie Fowler
*Camera:* William Mellor, L. B. Abbott
*Art directors:* Jack Martin Smith, Malcolm Brown
*Set directors:* Walter Scott, Stuart Reiss
*Costumes:* Dan Feld
*Makeup:* Ben Nye
*Sound:* Alfred Bruzlin, Warren Delaplain
*Second unit director:* William Whitney
*Running time:* 116 minutes

## HOW THE WEST WAS WON (MGM—1962)

*Directors:* Henry Hathaway, John Ford, George Marshall
*Producer:* Bernard Smith
*Cast:* (All the stars and superstars agreed to be listed alphabetically) Carroll
Baker, Lee J. Cobb, Henry Fonda, Carolyn Jones, Karl Malden, Gregory
Peck, George Peppard, Robert Preston, Debbie Reynolds, James Stewart,
Eli Wallach, John Wayne, Richard Widmark, Brigid Bazlen, Walter
Brennan, David Brian, Andy Devine, Raymond Massey, Agnes Moore-
head, Henry Morgan, Thelma Ritter, Mickey Shaughnessy, Russ Tam-
blyn
*Narrator:* Spencer Tracy
*Screenplay:* James R. Webb
*Assistant directors:* George Marshall, Jr., William McGarry, Robert Saun-
ders
*Music:* Alfred Newman, Ken Darby
*Editor:* Harold Kress
*Camera:* William Daniels, Milton Krasner, Charles Lang, Jr., Joseph La
Shelle, Harold Wellman
*Art directors:* George Davis, William Ferrari, Addison Hehr
*Set directors:* Henry Grace, Don Greenwood, Jr., Jack Mills
*Costumes:* Walter Plunkett
*Running time:* 155 minutes

# TAKE HER, SHE'S MINE *(20th Century-Fox— 1963)*

*Director:* Henry Koster
*Producer:* Henry Koster
*Cast:* James Stewart, Sandra Dee, Audrey Meadows, Robert Morley, John McGiver, Philippe Forquet, Robert Denver, Monica Moran, Jenny Maxwell, Cynthia Pepper, Irene Isu, Maurice Marsac, Charles Doherty, Marcel Hillaire, Charles Robinson, Janine Grandel, Marie Baker
*Authors:* Phoebe and Henry Ephron
*Screenplay:* Nunnally Johnson
*Assistant director:* Joseph Rickards
*Music:* Jerry Goldsmith
*Orchestrator:* Arthur Morton
*Editor:* Marjorie Fowler
*Camera:* Lucien Ballard
*Art directors:* Jack Martin Smith, Malcolm Brown
*Set directors:* Walter Scott, Stuart Reiss
*Costumes:* Travilla
*Makeup:* Ben Nye
*Sound:* W. D. Flick
*Special effects:* L. B. Abbott, Emil Kosa, Jr.
*Running time:* 98 minutes

## CHEYENNE AUTUMN *(Warner Brothers—1964)*

*Director:* John Ford
*Producer:* Bernard Smith
*Cast:* James Stewart, Edward G. Robinson, Richard Widmark, Carroll Baker, Karl Malden, Sal Mineo, Dolores Del Rio, Arthur Kennedy, Ricardo Montalban, Gilbert Roland, John Carradine, Victor Jory, George O'Brien, Patrick Wayne, Elizabeth Allen, Ben Johnson, Harry Carey, Jr.
*Author:* Mari Sandoz
*Screenplay:* James R. Webb
*Associate director:* Ray Kellogg
*Assistant directors:* Wingate Smith, Russ Saunders
*Music:* Alex North
*Editor:* Otho Lovering
*Camera:* William Clothier
*Art director:* Richard Day
*Set director:* Darrell Silvera
*Sound:* Francis Stahl
*Running time:* 156 minutes

## DEAR BRIGITTE *(20th Century-Fox—1965)*

*Director:* Henry Koster
*Producer:* Henry Koster, Fred Kohlmar
*Cast:* James Stewart, Fabian, Glynis Johns, Ed Wynn, Cindy Carol, Billy Mumy, John Williams, Jack Kruschen, Charles Robinson, Howard Freeman, Jane Wald, Alice Pearce, Jesse White, Gene O'Donnell, Brigitte Bardot
*Author:* John Hasse
*Screenplay:* Hal Kanter
*Assistant director:* Fred R. Simpson
*Music:* George Duning
*Orchestrator:* Arthur Morton
*Editor:* Marjorie Fowler
*Camera:* Lucien Ballard
*Art directors:* Jack Martin Smith, Malcolm Brown
*Set directors:* Walter Scott, Steve Potter
*Costumes:* Moss Mabry
*Makeup:* Ben Nye
*Sound:* Alfred Buzlin, Elmer Kosa, Jr.
*Special effects:* L. B. Abbott
*Running time:* 100 minutes

## *SHENANDOAH (Universal—1965)*

**Director:** Andrew V. McLaglen
**Producer:** Robert Arthur
**Cast:** James Stewart, Doug McClure, Glenn Corbett, Patrick Wayne, Rosemary Forsyth, Phillip Alford, Katharine Ross, Charles Robinson, James McMullan, Tim McIntyre, Eugene Jackson, Jr., Paul Fix, Denver Pyle, George Kennedy, Strother Martin, James Best, Tom Simcox, Berkeley Harris, Harry Carey, Jr., Kelvin Hagen, Dabbs Greer, Kelly Thordsen, Howard Faulkner
**Screenplay:** James Lee Barrett
**Music:** Frank Skinner
**Musical director:** Joseph Gershenson
**Editor:** Otho Lovering
**Camera:** William Clothier
**Art directors:** Alexander Golitzen, Alfred Sweeney
**Set directors:** John McCarthy, Oliver Emert
**Costumes:** Rosemary Odell
**Sound:** William O. Watson
**Running time:** 105 minutes

# THE FLIGHT OF THE PHOENIX
## *(20th Century-Fox— 1965)*

*Director:* Robert Aldrich
*Producer:* Robert Aldrich
*Cast:* James Stewart, Richard Attenborough, Peter Finch, Hardy Kruger, Ernest Borgnine, Dan Duryea, George Kennedy, Ian Bannen, Ronald Fraser, Christian Marquand, Gabriele Tinti, Alex Montoya, Peter Bravos, William Aldrich, Barrie Chase
*Author:* Elleston Trevor
*Screenplay:* Lukas Heller
*Assistant directors:* William Sheehan, Cliff Coleman, Alan Callow
*Music:* Frank De Vol
*Orchestrator:* Al Woodbury
*Editor:* Frank Luciano
*Camera:* Joseph Biroc
*Art director:* William Glasgow
*Set director:* Lucian Hafley
*Costumes:* Norma Koch
*Makeup:* Ben Nye
*Special effects:* L. B. Abbott, Howard Lydecker
*Running time:* 147 minutes

# THE RARE BREED (Universal—1966)

**Director:** Andrew V. McLaglen
**Producer:** William Alland
**Cast:** James Stewart, Maureen O'Hara, Brian Keith, Juliet Mills, David Brian, Don Galloway, Jack Elam, Ben Johnson, Harry Carey, Jr., Perry Lopez, Larry Domasin, Alan Caillou, Bob Gravage
**Screenplay:** Ric Hardman
**Assistant director:** Terry Morse, Jr.
**Music:** Johnny Williams
**Musical director:** Joseph Gershenson
**Editor:** Russell Schoengarth
**Camera:** William Clothier
**Art directors:** Alexander Golitzen, Alfred Ybarra
**Set directors:** John McCarthy, Oliver Emert
**Costumes:** Rosemary Odell
**Makeup:** Bud Westmore
**Running time:** 105 minutes

## *FIRECREEK (Warner Brothers—1968)*

*Director:* Vincent McEveety
*Producer:* Philip Leacock
*Cast:* James Stewart, Henry Fonda, Inger Stevens, Gary Lockwood, Dean
 •Jagger, Ed Begley, Jay C. Flippen, Jack Elam, James Best, J. Robert Por-
 ter, Morgan Woodward, Althena Lorde, John Qualen, Louise Latham,
 Slim Duncan, Kevin Tate, Christopher Shea
*Screenplay:* Calvin Clements
*Assistant director:* Jack Cunningham
*Music:* Alfred Newman
*Editor:* William Ziegler
*Camera:* William Clothier
*Art director:* Howard Hollander
*Set director:* William Kuehl
*Costumes:* Yvonne Wood
*Makeup:* Gordon Bau
*Sound:* Stanley Jones
*Running time:* 104 minutes

## *BANDOLERO! (20th Century-Fox—1968)*

*Director:* Andrew V. McLaglen
*Producer:* Robert L. Jacks
*Cast:* James Stewart, Dean Martin, Raquel Welch, George Kennedy,
 Andrew Prine, Will Geer, Clint Ritchie, Denver Pyle, Tom Heaton,
 Rudy Diaz, Sean McClory, Guy Raymond, Jock Mahoney
*Author:* Stanley Hough
*Screenplay:* James Lee Barrett
*Assistant director:* Terry Morse, Jr.
*Music:* Jerry Goldsmith
*Orchestrator:* Herbert Spencer
*Editor:* Folmar Blangsted
*Camera:* William Clothier
*Art directors:* Jack Martin Smith, Alfred Sweeney, Jr.
*Set directors:* Walter Scott, Chester Bayhi
*Makeup:* Dan Striepeke
*Sound:* Herman Lewis, David Dockendorf
*Special effects:* L. B. Abbott, Emil Kosa, Jr.
*Running time:* 107 minutes

177

# THE CHEYENNE SOCIAL CLUB
## (National General— 1970)

*Director:* Gene Kelly
*Executive producer:* James Lee Barrett
*Producer:* Gene Kelly
*Cast:* James Stewart, Henry Fonda, Shirley Jones, Elaine Devry, Robert
   Middleton, Arch Johnson, Dabbs Greer, Jackie Russell, Jackie Joseph,
   Sharon DeBord, Richard Collier, Charles Tyner, Jean Willes, Robert
   Wilke, Carl Reindel, Jason Wingreen
*Screenplay:* James Lee Barrett
*Assistant director:* Paul A. Helmick
*Music:* Walter Scharf
*Editor:* Adrienne Fazan
*Camera:* William Clothier
*Art director:* Gene Allen
*Set director:* George Hopkins
*Makeup:* Frank Westmore
*Sound:* Fred Faust
*Running time:* 103 minutes

# *FOOL'S PARADE (Columbia—1971)*

**Director:** Andrew V. McLaglen
**Producer:** Andrew V. McLaglen
**Associate producer:** Harry Bernsen
**Cast:** James Stewart, George Kennedy, Anne Baxter, Strother Martin, Kurt Russell, William Windom, Kathy Cannon, Robert Donner, Mike Kellin, Morgan Paul, David Huddleston, Dort Clark
**Author:** Davis Grubb
**Screenplay:** James Lee Barrett
**Assistant director:** Howard Koch, Jr.
**Music:** Harry Vars
**Editors:** David Bretherton, Robert Simpson
**Camera:** Harry Stradling, Jr.
**Art director:** Alfred Sweeney
**Set director:** Marvin March
**Costumes:** Guy Verhille
**Makeup:** Frank Westmore, Hank Edds
**Sound:** Al Overton, Jr.
**Special effects:** Charles Gasper
**Running time:** 90 minutes

# *THAT'S ENTERTAINMENT (MGM—1974)*

*Director:* Jack Haley, Jr.
*Executive producer:* Daniel Melnick
*Producer:* Jack Haley, Jr.
*Narrators:* Fred Astaire, Bing Crosby, Gene Kelly, Peter Lawford, Liza
  Minnelli, Donald O'Connor, Debbie Reynolds, Mickey Rooney, Frank
  Sinatra, James Stewart, Elizabeth Taylor
*Screenplay:* Jack Haley, Jr.
*Assistant directors:* Richard Bremerkamp, David Silver, Claude Bingon, Jr.
*Music supervisor:* Jesse Kaye
*Additional music:* Henry Mancini
*Head film librarian:* Mort Feinstein
*Optical supervision:* Robert Hoag, Jim Liles
*Camera:* Gene Polito, Ernest Laszlo, Russell Metty, Ennio Guarnieri, Allan
  Green
*Film editors:* Bud Friedgen, David Blewill
*Running time:* 127 minutes

# THE SHOOTIST *(Paramount—1976)*

*Director:* Don Siegel
*Executive producer:* Dino De Laurentiis
*Producers:* M. J. Frankovich, William Self
*Cast:* John Wayne, Lauren Bacall, Ron Howard, James Stewart, Richard Boone, Hugh O'Brian, Harry Morgan, Bill McKinney, John Carradine, Sheree North, Richard Lenz, Scatman Crothers
*Author:* Glendon Swarthout
*Screenplay:* Miles Hood Swarthout, Scott Hale
*Assistant directors:* Joe Cavalier, Joe Florence
*Music:* Elmer Bernstein
*Editor:* Douglas Stewart
*Camera:* Bruce Surtees
*Art director:* Robert Boyle
*Set director:* Arthur Parker
*Sound:* Alfred J. Overton
*Special effects:* Augie Lohman
*Running time:* 100 minutes

## *AIRPORT 77 (Universal— 1977)*

*Director:* Jerry Jameson
*Executive producer:* Jennings Lang
*Producer:* William Frye
*Cast:* James Stewart, Jack Lemmon, Olivia de Havilland, Lee Grant, Joseph
  Cotten, Brenda Vaccaro, Darren McGavin, Christopher Lee, George
  Kennedy, Tom Sullivan, Kathleen Quinlan, Pamela Bellwood, James
  Booth, Betty Parsons, Robert Foxworth, Monica Lewis, M. Emmet
  Walsh, Gil Garard, Mike Fingers
*Screenplay:* David Spector, Michael Scheff
*Assistant directors:* Wilbur Mosier, Bog Graner, Jim Nasella
*Second unit director:* Michael Moore
*Editor:* Terry Williams
*Camera:* Philip Lathrop
*Second unit camera:* Rex Metz
*Art director:* George Webb
*Set director:* Mickey Michaels
*Costumes:* Edith Head
*Sound:* Darin Knight
*Special effects:* Whitney McMahan, Frank Brendel
*Running time:* 129 minutes

## THE BIG SLEEP (United Artists—1978)

**Director:** Michael Winner
**Producers:** Elliott Kastner, Michael Winner
**Cast:** Robert Mitchum, Sarah Miles, Richard Boone, Candy Clark, Joan Collins, Edward Fox, John Mills, James Stewart, Oliver Reed, Harry Andrews
**Author:** Raymond Chandler
**Screenplay:** Michael Winner
**Editor:** Freddie Wilson
**Camera:** Robert Paynter
**Running time:** 100 minutes

## THE MAGIC OF LASSIE (Lassie Productions—1978)

**Director:** Don Chaffey
**Producers:** Bonita Granville Wrather, William Beaudine, Jr.
**Cast:** James Stewart, Mickey Rooney, Alice Faye, Pernell Roberts, Stephanie Zimbalist, Michael Sharrett, Lane Davies, Mike Mazurki
**Screenplay:** Jean Holloway, Robert B. Sherman, Richard Sherman
**Running time:** 90 minutes

# INDEX

187

JHAN ROBBINS

Grady, Bill (casting director), on J. S.'s
military service, 35, 51, 52, 56, 65
Granger, Farley, 85
Grant, Cary, 49, 64
Grauman's Chinese Theater, and J. S.'s
handprints, 62
*Greatest Show on Earth, The* (film), 94, 154

Haight, George, 30
Harding, Warren G., 22
Harlow, Jean, 63
as "good kisser," 38
Hart, Moss, 43
*Harvey* (film), 11–12, 93, 152
*Harvey* (play), 93
Hastings, Bill, on J. S., 54
Hathaway, Henry, 120
*Hawkins* (TV miniseries), 111–12, 113
Hayes (Will) office, 46
Hayward, Brooke, 38
Hayward, Leland, 56, 68, 95, 122
Henderson, Archie (popcorn salesman),
62
Hendricks, Ken, on J. S. and Boy
Scouts, 118–19
Hepburn, Katharine, 49, 113
see also *Philadelphia Story, The*
Heston, Charlton, 94
Hitchcock, Alfred, 84–90, 93, 94, 119
J. S.'s admiration for, 84
Hoffman, Dustin, 122–23
Hoover, Herbert, 25
J. S.'s defense of, 26
Hope, Bob, 103
Hopper, Hedda, 34–35
Howard, John, 49
Hudson, Rock, 123
J. S. as cowboy, 78
Huston, Walter, 42

*Ice Follies of 1939* (film), 44, 98, 138
Indiana, Pennsylvania (J. S.'s home
town), 14–15
Indiana University, Pennsylvania, 15
*It's a Wonderful Life* (film), 12, 58–59, 60,
145
*It's a Wonderful World* (film), 44, 139

Jarvis, Abraham, 18
*Jezebel* (film), 50
*Jimmy Stewart Show, The* (TV series), 110–
11
"Jimmy Stewart Sound-Alike Contest,"
42–43

*Journey by Night* (play), J. S.'s mishaps in,
32–33

Karp, David, 112
Kaufman, George S., 43
Kazan, Elia, 120
Kelly, Grace, 87
on Hitchcock and J. S., 84–85
Kennedy Center, award to J. S., 120–21
Khan, Princess Yasmin, 123
Kilgallen, Dorothy, 110
Kingsley, Sidney, 31
*King's Row* (film), 107
Kirkpatrick, Steve (bomber squadron
navigator), on J. S., 55
Koster, Henry, 94, 98, 120

La Guardia, Fiorello, 119
Lamarr, Hedy, 49
Lamour, Dorothy, 94
*Last Gangster, The* (film), 41, 134
LeRoy, Mervyn, 97
Lewis, William C., Jr., 117
Liberty Films, 58, 60
Lindbergh, Charles A., 21
meeting with J. S., 95–96
see also *Spirit of St. Louis*
Livanos, George, 123
Livingston, Mary (Mrs. Jack Benny),
102
Logan, Joshua, 27, 33, 100
on J. S. as actor, 29, 65–66
Lombard, Carole, 43–44
Lombardi, Sal (Princeton shoemaker),
25–26
Loomis, Don (body builder), and under-
weight problems of J. S., 36–37
Los Angeles Area Scout Council, 118–19
Loy, Myrna, 38, 40

McClintic, Guthrie, 34
McCormick, Myron, 27, 33, 100
MacDonald, Jeanette, 37
McLean, Edward, Jr. (first husband
of Gloria Stewart), 69
McLean, Evelyn Walsh, 69
McLean, Gloria Hatrick, *see* Stewart,
Gloria
McLean, Michael (stepson), 73–75, 116
McLean, Ronald (stepson), 73–75, 76
death in Vietnam, 116–17
MacMurray, Fred, 110
McNair, Everett, 17
*Made for Each Other* (film), 44, 138

189